Life inside the Cloister

KADOC STUDIES ON RELIGION, CULTURE & SOCIETY 21

Thomas Coomans

LIFE INSIDE THE CLOISTER

Understanding Monastic Architecture: Tradition, Reformation, Adaptive Reuse

Leuven University Press

This book appears in the peer-reviewed series
KADOC Studies on Religion, Culture & Society

Cover: Former Celestine Priory in Leuven (Belgium), converted into the Library of Sciences and Technology at the University of Leuven by architect Rafael Moneo in 1996-2002.
[© THOC]

ISBN 978 94 6270 143 4
D/2018/1869/24
NUR: 704

GPRC Guaranteed Peer Reviewed Content www.gprc.be

fwo Research Foundation Flanders Opening new horizons

RLICC

CONTENTS

INTRODUCTION

UNDERSTANDING MONASTIC ARCHITECTURE

Life and Afterlife inside the Cloister

The first objective of this book is to understand the architecture of monasteries and convents as a process of the tangible and symbolic organisation of space and time for religious communities subject to regulated lives. Despite the weight of age-old and seemingly immutable monastic tradition, architecture has played a part in the adaptation of different forms of regular religious life to the changing needs of society and the Church, while favouring the affirmation of strong and specific religious identities in an apostolic and evangelising spirit.

The second objective concerns the afterlife of the architecture of monasteries and convents in a Western society 'exculturated of Catholicism'.[1] This is a highly topical issue. Many religious communities that have not recruited for several decades find themselves having to leave their monastery or convent. 'These religious properties still hold a strategic position in the regional landscape or urban fabric, dominating the collective memory and imagination. As a result, the houses of the religious are being coveted.'[2]

Monasteries and convents offer conversion opportunities that differ greatly from those of parish churches, whether heritagised or not, which are

1 Hervieu-Léger, *Catholicisme, la fin d'un monde.*

2 Noppen, Coomans and Drouin, eds, *Des couvents en heritage / Religious Houses: A Legacy*, 6.

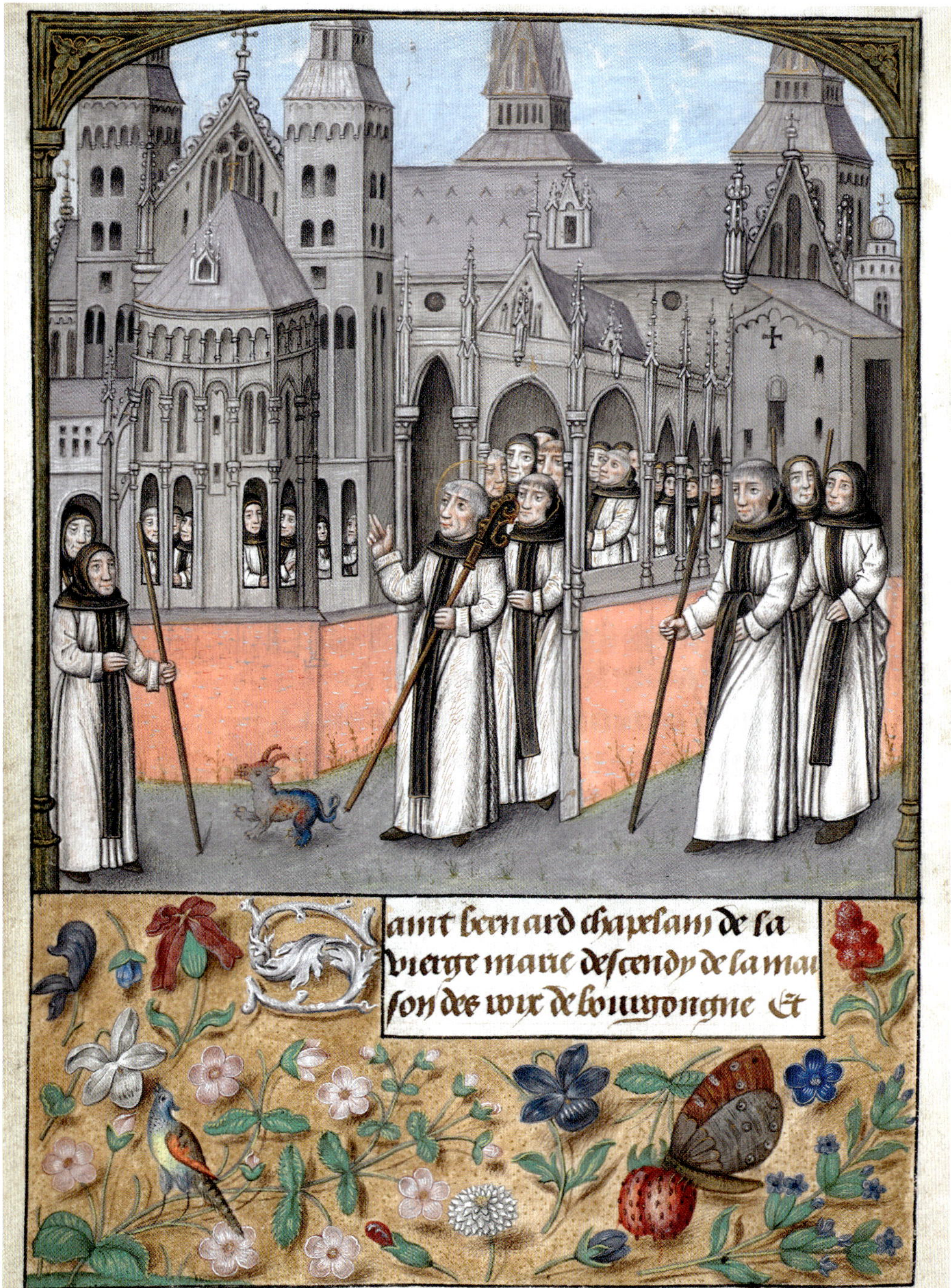

Fig. 1. Saint Bernard Abbot and his community of Cistercian monks, manuscript illumination from *Burgundy Chronicle* (MS Yates Thompson, 32, f. 9v), fifteenth century.
[© London, British Library]

also under pressure in Western societies.[3] The main reason for this is their architectural configuration, which consists of several buildings arranged around a cloister or courtyard and is generally inward-looking or separate from the outside world. It is for this reason that the cloister is the focal point of this book, because it is both architecture, a physical reality, and a metaphor for the religious life that takes place within it. [Fig. 1]

How can the spirit, or intangible heritage of life inside the cloister be perpetuated after the departure of the religious community? What is the value of such sacred heritage in today's society? These questions lie at the very heart of the process of heritage adaptive reuse and the success of an architectural project depends on the answers to them.

2018, the European Year of Cultural Heritage, has chosen religious heritage as one of the three key heritage focus – together with industrial and military heritage – for its action. Adaptive reuse is one of its specific objectives: 'to promote debate, research and the exchange of good practices on the quality of conservation, safeguarding, innovative reuse and enhancement of cultural heritage, and on contemporary interventions in the historical environment'.[4]

Our students from the Advanced Master in Conservation of Monuments and Sites feel quite out of their depth whenever they are faced with a heritage value assessment of a monastery as part of their projects and dissertations.[5] Often, they have no image of an abbey or a monastery other than that on the beer, liquor, cheese or chocolate packaging that bears its name. Despite sound architectural, historical, technical and pathological knowledge, a heritage value assessment of a monastery without an understanding of religious life or the significance behind monastic architecture cannot lead to a successful heritage adaptive reuse as it likely overlooks key elements. This book is not only targeted at students and project architects but at all those seeking to understand monastic architecture beyond the beauty of its stones and its richness of styles. Contextual understanding of monastic architecture is essential to understanding life and afterlife inside the cloister.

The choice made by both men and women alike to withdraw from the world and renounce temporal goods to live in solitude, poverty and contemplation can be found in most human societies and religions, including Buddhism, Islam and all Christian confessions, Orthodox, Roman Catholic and even Reformed Churches. We will limit ourselves to Western Christianity, however, to Catholicism in particular, because it is the architecture of Catholic

3 Morisset, Noppen and Coomans, eds, *Quel avenir pour quelles églises? / What Future for Which Churches?*

4 Decision (EU) 2017/864 of the European Parliament and of the Council of 17 May 2017 on a European Year of Cultural Heritage (2018), article 2.2.c. <http://eur-lex.europa.eu/eli/dec/2017/864/oj>.

5 KU Leuven, Raymond Lemaire International Centre for Conservation <http://set.kuleuven.be/rlicc>.

Fig. 2. Religious orders, female dress, historical overview, after the Franciscan father Hippolyte Hélyot, Paris: Basset, mid-nineteenth century.
[© KIK-IRPA, Brussels / Jean-Luc Elias]

monasticism in Western Europe – and to a lesser extent in North America – that is faced with deconsecration and reuse. The architecture of monasteries and convents built by missionary societies in Latin America, Africa and Asia is not discussed here but can be understood using a similar approach to that developed in the first three sections of this book.

The Sacred and the Material

To the question 'What makes a monastery a sacred place?' Dom Armand Veilleux, Abbot of the Trappist abbey of Scourmont, gives a clear answer:

> Monastic architecture (...) is sacred not because it is built in such and such a way, because it is old or even because it is beautiful. It is sacred simply because of what is lived (or has been lived) there. Of course some of those buildings are masterpieces of architecture and of art – thank God. But that does not make them more sacred and holier than any simple, even un-artistic or contemporary monastic building.
>
> Monasteries are sacred because they are inhabited by women or men who want to make their lives a worship of God. Some of them may be holy people, others not. What makes a sacred place of their place is the holiness of the spiritual goal they have chosen for their lives. To what

Fig. 3. Religious orders, male dress, historical overview, after the Franciscan father Hippolyte Hélyot, Paris: Basset, mid-nineteenth century.
[© KADOC, Leuven]

> extent they attain that goal and to what extent they fall short of it is another question – and an important question for sure – but one which has no impact on the holiness or sacredness of the place.[6]

There is no need to explore the theological, philosophical and anthropological approaches to the sacred or various different types of sacred places and their cultural significance here; there is plenty of literature on this subject.[7] This book does not offer a broad historical overview of Christian monasticism through the centuries and only briefly touches on the terminology and complexity of religious orders, congregations and institutes past and present, of which there are several thousand! [Figs 2-3] There are sufficient encyclopaedias, directories and websites that discuss, to a more or less exhaustive extent, the various monastic movements, their rules, reforms and dissemination, as well as the details of their spirituality and liturgy.[8] Moreover, monasticism and religious orders occupy a significant proportion of dictionaries and

6 Veilleux, 'What makes a Monastery a Sacred Place?', 30.

7 Notably: Coomans et al., eds, *Loci Sacri: Understanding Sacred Places.*

8 Johnston, ed., *Encyclopedia of Monasticism*; Laboa, ed., *The Historical Atlas of Eastern and Western Monasticism*; Le Bras, ed., *Les orders religieux*; Lobrichon, *Les moines d'Occident*; De Maeyer, Leplae and Schmiedl, eds, *Religious Institutes in Western Europe*; and: <http://kadoc.kuleuven.be/relins/be/>; Hélyot and Bullot, *Histoire des ordres monastiques religieux et militaires*; Altermatt et al., *Religious Institutes.*

encyclopaedias of Christianity.[9] Medieval monasticism in particular continues to attract considerable interest from researchers.[10]

It is the architecture, or the 'built environment' in its concrete tangibility and heritage dimension that serves as our starting point and makes this book original. How, starting from the architectural elements, can we trace their use back to what was (or is) a combination of spiritual and tangible dimensions? The question of use leads inevitably to the question of use value that is central to the context of all heritage conversions.[11] It is through architecture that the great religious families and milestones appear in a chronology that extends over more than seventeen centuries.

As a result of the pioneering work of Viollet-le-Duc (1854) and the first generation of archaeologists, studies and publications on monastic and religious architecture are extremely diverse.[12] *Monasteries of Western Europe. The Architecture of the Orders* by Wolfgang Braunfels (1972) remains an overview of quality despite the author's lack of interest in the nineteenth and twentieth centuries and the absence of the issue of adaptive reuse.[13] Since Braunfels, the field has expanded considerably and been enriched by countless monographic, archaeological and architectural studies. Overviews, nevertheless, either come up short or are limited to a single religious order, country, style, type of building (churches in particular) or period.[14] The architecture of certain orders, such as the Benedictines, Cistercians and Jesuits, and to a lesser extent that of mendicant orders and the Carthusians, receives much more attention than that of others, of female orders in particular.[15] Only medieval and Baroque abbeys and monasteries appear on the UNESCO World Heritage list.[16] The inclusion of the neo-Gothic beguinage of Sint-Amandsberg in 1998 and Le Corbusier's La Tourette friary in 2016 are the exceptions that confirm the rule, but they are both part of serial nominations.

9 *New Catholic Encyclopedia*; Betz et al., eds, *Religion Past and Present*; *Dictionnaire d'histoire et de géographie ecclésiastiques.*

10 Several specialised journals (*Monastic Studies*; *Journal of Medieval Monastic Studies*; *Revue Bénédictine*; *Cîteaux commentarii cistercienses*; and many others) as well as numerous books. Amongst other works: Lawrence, *Medieval Monasticism*; Brooke, *The Age of the Cloister*; Gleba, *Klosterleben im Mittelalter*; Melville, Schneidmüller and Weinfurter, eds, *Innovationen durch Deuten und Gestalten*; Burton and Stöber, eds, *Women in the Medieval Monastic World.*

11 Noppen and Morisset, *Les églises du Québec*, 321-335 ('la valeur d'usage des églises: du sacré au sacral'); Riegl, 'The Modern Cult of Monuments'.

12 Viollet-le-Duc, *Dictionnaire raisonné*, vol. 1, 241-312; Coppack, *Abbeys and Priories*, 12-20.

13 Braunfels, *Monasteries of Western Europe.*

14 Binding and Untermann, *Kleine Kunstgeschichte der mittelalterlichen Ordensbaukunst*; Klein, ed., *Der mittelalterliche Kreuzgang*; O'Malley and Bailey, eds, *The Jesuits and the Arts*; Navascués Palacio, *Monasterios en España*; Schütz, *Abbayes et monastères d'Europe*; Toman, *Monasteries and Monastic Orders*, etc.

15 See footnotes 58 to 119.

16 <http://whc.unesco.org/en/list>.

Nineteenth- and twentieth-century monasteries and convents, both for men and women, with the exception of certain iconic monasteries of modern architecture, are the poor relations in the history of architecture. Paradoxically, they constitute a much larger number of sites and buildings and are therefore the most under threat. This lack of study results in a lack of knowledge and a greater struggle for heritage recognition, even unsuccessful reuse and destruction. In Québec, a province without medieval architecture but extremely rich in nineteenth- and twentieth-century religious houses, have studies and interest in this kind of heritage been seen since the 1970s.[17] In Europe, pioneering historical research has recently investigated the economic history of religious orders and congregations from the 1770s to 1930, with a focus on their management, finances and patrimony.[18] Architectural projects and real estate strategies are an integral part of the economic and material history of a religious community. This is particularly obvious when an architectural monastic complex is sold to developers. In such extreme circumstances, the balance among the sacred and material is totally disrupted.

Structure and Background

Approaching the architecture of a monastery or convent through its cloister allows it to be considered as a whole. In this way it becomes less about churches and more about the morphology of monasteries, their organisation around the cloister and their evolution. The central space of a monastery, the cloister has always been the focus of attention for its occupants. It is also the cloister and its courtyard garden that bestow a unique architectural added-value on a reused monastery.

This book is divided into four sections and 26 short chapters:

- The first section deals with the origins of monasticism and monastic architecture. How, after several centuries, was space organised appropriately around the cloister, cell and church? What was the role of the Rule in community life?
- The second section examines different architectural types. How, in essence, did the architecture of monasteries and religious institutes respond to the identity of the major religious families, according to a rule and an apostolate, in other words to their profound identities? Nine types of architecture are described thereafter: the abbey, the charterhouse, the castle, the mendicant friary, the beguinage, the Hôtel-Dieu or hospital, the college, the palace and the house monastery.

17 Drouin, 'La sauvegarde des édifices conventuels'; Noppen and Morisset, 'La renaissance des couvents au Québec'; Noppen and Morisset, *Les églises du Québec*.

18 Van Dijck and De Maeyer, eds, *The Economics of Providence*.

- The third section is devoted to characters that embody the sacred and affect, in one way or another, all monasteries and religious houses. How can the evolution of monastic architecture over space and time be explained, taking into account different identities and contexts? Six characters are analysed: place and stability, enclosure and gender, liturgy and identity, death and memory, scale and growth, and finally, style.
- The fourth and final section questions the future of monasteries after the departure of the faithful and outlines a typology of the reuse of monasteries. Besides destruction and ruin, what are the other possible uses of monastic architecture? Agricultural, industrial, residential, penal, military, educational and cultural. It will become apparent that the issues presented by other uses are not a new phenomenon.

Neither the examples cited nor the illustrations are by any means exhaustive as Europe is home to thousands of monasteries, abbeys, convents and other religious houses. The choice is the result of earlier study, publications, visits and travel. This has evolved according to our research projects, beginning with a monograph of the Cistercian abbey of Villers (Belgium), followed by the architecture of Cistercians, Mendicants and Beguines in the former Low Countries, before moving onto the nineteenth century and the Gothic Revival of the Saint Luke Schools, restorations, issues of heritagisation and adaptive reuse in Europe and Quebec, and finally, East Asia and the Jesuits in China.[19]

Acknowledgements

Planning for this book began with a major conference held on 8 October 2009 at the Belles Soirées at the Université de Montréal, as part of the symposium *Des couvents en heritage / Religious Houses: A Legacy* organised by the *Chaire de recherche du Canada en patrimoine urbain* / Canada Research Chair in Urban Heritage (UQAM – Université du Québec à Montréal). I am most grateful to Prof. Luc Noppen and to Prof. Lucie K. Morisset, the two successive holders of the Research Chair, for involving me in this symposium and the resulting reference publication. Once reworked, the text of my lecture became a substantial chapter.[20] Written in 2010, during my fellowship at the Netherlands Institute for Advanced Study in the Humanities and Social Sciences, this text was published in 2015. In the meantime, the issue of the future of religious heritage suddenly became more pressing in Europe.

19 Coomans, 'Entrevista'.

20 Thomas Coomans, 'L'ordre autour du cloître: l'architecture des abbayes et des couvents entre tradition, réformes et réaffectations' in: Luc Noppen, Thomas Coomans and Martin Drouin, eds, *Des couvents en héritage / Religious Houses: A Legacy*. Patrimoine urbain 15. Québec: Presses de l'Université du Québec, 2015, 13-109 [ISBN: 978-2-7605-4354-6].

The opportunity to publish an enhanced and updated version of the Montreal chapter as a full book in English arose in 2016 in the context of our research project 'Redeveloping the city: urban transformation after the suppression of religious houses in Belgian towns at the dawn of the modern age (1773/1796-1860)', granted by the FWO Research Foundation-Flanders.[21]

I would like to thank Prof. Luc Noppen, Prof. Martin Drouin, as well as the Presses de l'Université du Québec, in particular Martine Des Rochers, General Manager, and Martine Pelletier, Publishing Manager, for their authorisation. Our gratitude also goes to KADOC - Documentation and Research Center on Religion, Culture and Society, and in particular to Prof. Jan De Maeyer and Luc Vints, for agreeing to include the publication in the KADOC Studies on Religion, Culture and Society series, as well as to Dr. Veerle De Laet, director of University Press Leuven, and to Laura Bennett for the English translation.

I am also grateful to Prof. David N. Bell, Prof. Anna Bergmans, Prof. Wim Blockmans, Prof. Caroline Bruzelius, Prof. Krista De Jonge, Prof. Dirk Jan de Vries, Prof. Luc Francis Genicot (†), Prof. Tony Hackens (†), Prof. Ho Puay-peng, Prof. Terryl N. Kinder, Prof. Jean-Michel Leniaud, Prof. Aart Mekking, Prof. Wolfgang Schenkluhn and Prof. Éliane Vergnolle, who, at one time or another in my academic career, have stimulated aspects of my research relating to this publication. I would also like to mention the board members of the journal *Cîteaux commentarii cistercienses*, Lilian Grootswagers and the Council members of *Future for Religious Heritage*, Véronique Cardon, Stéphanie Coomans, Dr. Vincent Debonne, Dr. Peter Heyrman, Reinout Klaarenbeek, Dr. Willemijne Linssen, Tine Neskens, Oswald Pauwels, Philippe Pepermans, François Terlinden (†), Dr. Jeroen Westerman and Dr. Shu Changxue.

Finally, I would like to thank all the fathers, brothers and sisters who have welcomed me into their communities and shared their architectural experiences with me, in particular: Father Emmanuel André SJ (†), Father Josy Birsens SJ, Dom Pierre-André Burton OCSO, Sister Marie-Ignace Coomans de Brachène OSB (†), Brother Thierry de Béthune OSB, Dom Frédéric Debuyst OSB (†), Dom François de Place OCSO, Dom Daniel Misonne OSB, Brother Tarcies Morjeau O.Praem, Dom Michel Proulx O.Praem, Dom Armand Veilleux OCSO, and Father Armand Willot SJ (†).

21 FWO, G0B0912N, project co-promoted by Prof. Jan De Maeyer (KU Leuven), Prof. Inge Bertels (VUB, Brussels, presently UA, Antwerp), Prof. Tom Verschaffel (KULAK-KU Leuven) and Dr Peter Heyrman (KADOC-KU Leuven).

Fig. 4. Saint George Orthodox Monastery of Choziba in the Wadi Qelt (Palestine), founded in 480 AD for a community of hermits living in caves, re-established in the late nineteenth century. [© THOC]

ORIGINS
ORGANISING SACRED SPACE AND TIME

The origins of the monastic tradition and the architecture that accompanies it are the result of a long process that stretches from the first hermit communities of the third century to the Carolingian imperial abbeys of the ninth century. The origins and early development of monastic life are therefore essential to an understanding of the material and spiritual significance of the architecture. Living in a closed community, monks and nuns gave a symbolic or spiritual dimension to all the material components of the monastery, as well as to all the rituals that punctuated their daily lives. The organisation of the monastic space and the organisation of monastic time were sanctified and formed a whole in the service of a project for life that, in its essence and choices, aspired to divine perfection.

How, after several centuries, did the space of abbeys and monasteries become organised around the cloister? How did this spatial organisation become a monastic tradition? To answer these questions, we will examine the role of the Rule and organisation of the community, the two foundations of monastic life. The cell, church and cloister, the basic components required by devotional life in a monastery, are also addressed in the first section of this book. Other aspects, such as the choice of site and enclosure, are developed in the third section.

1. The Cell

The origin of Christian monasticism dates back to the late third century, in Egypt. A land of contrasts between the life concentrated in the Nile Valley and the surrounding desert on all sides, Egypt offered the chance to withdraw from the world.[22] Among those known as the 'desert fathers', the two most important were Anthony and Pachomius.[23] Saint Anthony the Great († circa 356) withdrew to the Nitrian Desert in around 270 and became the first of the great hermits, attracting many disciples around him. Latin tradition considers him the founder of monastic and eremitic life. Saint Pachomius († circa 349) founded communities of hermits in the Thebaid desert that obeyed a leader and lived in a sort of 'monastic village' surrounded by a wall, consisting of an oratory for praying and pavilions for working and sleeping. [Fig. 5] From 318, Pachomius founded several monasteries for men and women whose communities numbered several hundred members. To organise these communities, regulations or a monastic rule proved indispensable.[24] The Rule of Saint Pachomius was the first of its kind; according to tradition, Pachomius received it from an angel.

In the early fourth century, the Roman Empire converted to Christianity, which had developed from a dissident religion to a mass and then official religion. Starting in Egypt, the monastic movement spread across the Empire in the fourth and fifth centuries in two main directions: firstly, to the Near East, Syria, Arabia and Persia; and secondly, in Italy and Gaul, then to Ireland and England. The key stages of its spread to the West are the foundation in 339 of the first monastery in Rome by Saint Athanasius († 373), the foundation by Saint Martin († 397) of the first two monasteries in Gaul – in Ligugé near Poitiers in 361 and in Marmoutier in Tours in 375 – and the foundation by Saint Patrick († 461) of the first abbey in Ireland, in Armagh in 441.[25] A great many of the monasteries in the Near East and North Africa began to disappear from the seventh and eighth centuries onwards, following the development of Islam in these regions. The monasteries that survive in Egypt are Coptic Catholic or Eastern Orthodox. [Fig. 6]

The basic architectural component of eremitic and primitive monastic life was the cell. Regardless of its shape, the cell was by definition a small space – from the Latin *cellula*, a small chamber, the diminutive of *cella*, chamber – designed for one person. The first desert hermits withdrew to caves or tombs hollowed out of the mountain, or to abandoned villages. Later, a similar function was fulfilled by the monastic cells arranged along a corridor or the cell houses of the Carthusians [see Chapter 7].

22 Brooks Hedstrom, *The Monastic Landscape of Late Antique Egypt*.

23 Ward, *The Desert Fathers*; Gobry, *Les moines en Occident*, vol. 1; Gould, *The Desert Fathers on Monastic Community*.

24 About the daily life: Rousseau, *Pachomius: The Making of a Community*, 77-104.

25 Ryan, *Irish Monasticism*.

Fig. 5. Thebaide, scenes from the life of hermits, painting by Paolo Uccello, 1460s. [© Galleria dell'Accademia, Florence / Wikimedia Commons]

The monastic cell is the archetype of the relationship between material and spiritual that characterises monastic architecture and life. The cell is a closed room, devoid of any physical distraction, within which the member of the religious order is alone and in silence, away from the world and his or her community, to perform his or her spiritual tasks. This withdrawal from the world does not mean a rejection of the world. In fact, the cell is first and foremost the place where the monk or nun develops an inward-looking attitude conducive to finding him- or herself, with God and with others in an intense face-to-face, through prayer, meditation on the Bible, asceticism and work. This encounter with himself also gives rise to the monk's internal struggle with his desires and passions, with his ego, considered by the Desert Fathers and medieval monks or nuns to be the devil. The monastic cell can therefore perhaps be understood as a place of transformation and salvation, a place in which to discipline the body submitted to the mind. The cell gives form to the presence of God. This presence makes the space of the cell a sacred space, of which the monk or nun has to take care by rejecting any use that would violate its integrity.[26]

26 Keller, *Oasis of Wisdom*, 47-61.

2. The Rule

In principle, a hermit lived alone and organised himself as he pleased, but a community of hermits required a minimum of order to live together. Following the Rule of Saint Pachomius, a number of monastic rules or 'charters of life' were written during the first centuries of Christianity. Two of these were particularly successful and are pillars of life for religious communities still today: the Rule of Saint Augustine of Hippo, written at the very end of the fourth century, and the Rule of Saint Benedict of Nursia, from the mid-sixth century. In the early thirteenth century, the Rule of Saint Francis of Assisi founded another long-lasting tradition.

Saint Augustine († 430) was not a monk and the rule that bears his name is based on the precepts he wrote in 397 for a community in Hippo in Algeria.[27] This rule was adopted from the eleventh century by the communities of Canons, Premonstratensians, Dominicans and many other male and female orders and congregations who bear the name of Augustine.[28] The text says nothing about the architectural layout of the monastery and only makes mention of a specific building on one occasion: the oratory [see Chapter 4].

While the Roman Empire was cracking on all sides before collapsing in the sixth century under Barbarian invasions, monasticism developed in various forms.[29] It was in this context that Saint Benedict of Nursia († 547) wrote the 'Rule of Monks' for the community in Monte Cassino to the south of Rome.[30] This major work of the Christian monastic tradition is considered one of the most important texts of the Western Middle Ages.[31] In 73 chapters Saint Benedict described the various aspects that governed monastic life, ranging from the role of the abbot to liturgical prescriptions, community services, work, food, clothing, etc.

The Rule barely makes any mention of the architecture, or rather, the built environment in which the life of the monks took place. Besides the oratory, cited as a place but without architectural details, only one phrase relating to the surrounding enclosure and the role of the porter explicitly names buildings:

> If it can be done, the monastery should be so established that all the necessary things, such as water, mill, garden and various workshops,

27 Verheijen, *La Règle de Saint Augustin*.
28 Cocheril, 'L'ordre canonial'.
29 Dunn, *The Emergence of Monasticism*; Gobry, *Les moines en Occident*, vol. 2.
30 Amongst others: De Voguë, *Saint Benoît: l'homme et l'œuvre*; Cassanelli and Lopez-Tello Garcia, *Saint Benoît et son héritage artistique*.
31 There are numerous editions, comments and translations of Saint Benedict's Rule. We refer to the English translation by Father Leonard J. Doyle, 1948.

Fig. 6. Saint Catherine's Monastery at the foot of Mount Sinai (Egypt), built from 448 to 465.
[© Thierry Vermeeren]

> may be within the enclosure, so that there is no necessity for the monks to go about outside of it, since that is not at all profitable for their souls.[32]

This extract shows that the organisation of a community was based on order, as opposed to the chaos of the world, that order included the spatial layout of the monastery, and that the presence of an enclosure was the condition for the existence of such order. Moreover, in a monastery, 'a school for the service of the Lord and the amendment of vices or the preservation of charity',[33] all material considerations had both a spiritual and symbolic dimension.

In the mid-sixth century, the Rule of Saint Benedict was not the only rule of life. It resulted from a monastic tradition of several centuries and would, in turn, become a major reference in the monastic tradition right up until the present day, almost fifteen centuries later. Benedictine monasticism spread throughout Gaul, Germany and other regions that had been neither Romanised nor Christianised. Monasticism was no longer a world on the margins of

32 Benedict of Nursia, *Rule for Monasteries*, chapter 66.
33 Ibid., prologue.

Fig. 7. Monastery of Clonmacnoise (Ireland), founded in 544, ruined in 1552.
[© THOC]

society, as it was in the time of the Desert Fathers, but abbeys were gaining in power and influence thanks to the links they were forging with bishops, sovereigns and society. It was common for Benedictine abbots and monks to become bishops. The first pope of monastic origin was Saint Gregory the Great († 604), the father of the Western Church.

At the end of the sixth century, Benedictine monasticism came up against Irish monasticism, spread in the same regions of Northern Europe by Columbanus (†615), author of a rule that was stricter than that of Saint Benedict.[34] Benedictine monasticism gradually developed over the course of the eighth century, then, at the Council of Aachen in 817, the Carolingian emperor Louis the Pious imposed the Rule of Saint Benedict across the Empire to counteract the influence of Irish and Anglo-Saxon monks. The Rule of Saint Benedict owed its durability to the balance it offered between spiritual life (prayer, asceticism, poverty and chastity), manual work and intellectual culture. This balance was summed up by the famous Benedictine adage 'pray and work' (*ora et labora*).

The first five centuries of monasticism, outlined broadly here, took place in complex and often violent historical contexts, with the collapse of the Western Empire and Barbarian invasions, the development of Islam in North Africa and Spain, internal tensions within the Church, especially with the Christians of the East, and the evangelisation of new territories in Ireland and Central Europe. For monastic architecture before the Carolingian period, any knowledge

34 Gobry, *Les moines en Occident*, vol. 3.

we have is almost exclusively archaeological because the abbeys have all been destroyed or converted over the following centuries.

Based on the evidence of monastic ruins in Ireland, we must imagine monasteries surrounded by a circular enclosing wall and consisting of distinct buildings, made from wood and stone, in which the monks prayed, lived and worked together. [Fig. 7] Each abbey included several churches and chapels in which the liturgy alternated, depending on certain rituals and the relics of the saints kept there. There were no cloisters as yet therefore, but buildings detached from one another, most likely to avoid the spread of fire, and sometimes linked by galleries. Orthodox monasteries retained this layout, with multiple churches, an enclosure but no cloister.[35]

The rules of monastic life of Saint Benedict, Saint Augustine and Saint Francis were established as points of reference for the whole monastic world, but every order and religious institute had its own constitutions to which other normative documents, such as those of customs and internal regulations, were added. Constitutions could be revised under exceptional circumstances, while customary rules and regulations adapted to local contexts could be revised whenever necessary to maintain good order within a community.

3. The Community

In the first chapter of the Rule, Saint Benedict reveals the complexity of the monastic landscape, making a distinction between four categories of monks:

> The first kind are the Cenobites: those who live in monasteries and serve under a rule and an Abbot. The second kind are the Anchorites or Hermits: (...) after long probation in a monastery (...) go out to the solitary combat of the desert. (...) The third kind of monks, a detestable kind, are the Sarabaites. These, not having been tested by any rule (...), they still keep faith with the world (...) as liars before God. (...) The fourth kind of monks are those called Gyrovagues. (...) Always on the move, with no stability, they indulge their own wills and succumb to the allurements of gluttony, and are in every way worse than the Sarabaites.[36]

Saint Benedict therefore considered the category of the Cenobites (from the Greek *koinos bios*, common life) as superior and gave it a rule to organise it, whatever its size or composition. The extract shows that monastic vocations were multiple, even within a community of Cenobites. Unlike the Gyrovagues, a monastic community was attached to a place and took a vow of stability [see Chapter 15].

35 Kometch, *Monastères russes*.
36 Benedict of Nursia, *Rule for Monasteries*, chapter 1.

The Rule of Saint Benedict grants a significant place to the role of the community's superior, whom he named 'abbot' (from the Syriac *apa*, father); 'abbess' for female communities. The abbot is responsible for the spiritual and material aspect of the community, which is required to be obedient to him. [Fig. 8] The abbot has to be a skilled psychologist, as his authority adapts to the character of each monk for the maintenance of order. He acts in the name of the community towards the outside world and has to manage inevitable conflicts with neighbours: the villages, local lord, prince, bishop and other abbots. In the Middle Ages, it was not uncommon for the abbot to have the rank of lord and dispense justice. The designation of the abbot has always been a crucial question for the community, which, in theory, elects its own superior. However, it was often the case that an abbot from outside the community was imposed either by the political power – the king or emperor [see Chapter 13] – or by the central authorities of the monastic order.

Another crucial question is the length of the abbot's term. Normally he is elected for life and only resigns when he no longer feel able to perform his duties. Other formulas exist, depending on the orders and the period, in particular that of renewable and non-renewable fixed-term appointments.

The superior of the community is not called 'abbot' in all religious orders and institutes; there are also 'priors', 'guardians', 'rectors', 'superiors', 'commanders', etc. Finally, at the head of centralised orders there is an 'abbot general', a 'father general', a 'grand master', etc. All these titles have female equivalents in female institutions.

The abbot is surrounded by a council of elders (*seniores*), whom he consults for important decisions. He is assisted by a prior (from the Latin *prior*, first), who is more specifically responsible for the spiritual order of the community and acts as a substitute for the superior whenever he is absent. The cellarer or treasurer is responsible for the material aspects of the monastery, in other words, finances, logistics, construction, estate, workers, etc.

The members of the community take vows or make promises whereby they commit themselves deliberately to God, the abbot or the abbess and the community. The generic terms 'monk' and 'nun' refer to any person who has taken a vow. The distinction between orders, congregations and institutes, as well as between monks, brothers etc. is based on the nature of the vows taken.[37] The Rule of Saint Benedict provides for 'vows of stability, moral conversion and obedience', which led to the famous trilogy of 'vows of obedience, poverty and chastity,' to which, depending on the orders, specific vows are added. The renunciation of money and personal property, as well as the carnal dimension of the body and sexual activity, constitute monastic asceticism.

37 The code of canon law from 1917 dedicates 200 canons to the religious communities. See: *The 1917 Pio-Benedictine Code of Canon Law*.

Fig. 8. Saint Bernard teaching to the community in the chapter house (above), Saint Bernard in his cell (below), manuscript illumination by Jean Fouquet in the Book of Hours of Étienne Chevalier, 1450s. [© Musée Condé, Chantilly / photo RMN-Grand Palais, René-Gabriel Ojéda]

Fig. 9. Refectory of the Cistercian nunnery of Port-Royal des Champs (France), after Louise-Magdeleine Horthemels, circa 1710.
[© Musée de Port-Royal des Champs, Magny-les-Hameaux / photo RMN-Grand Palais, Gérard Blot]

The regular monk or nun takes simple or temporary vows, then solemn or final vows that commit him or her for life with legal canonical consequences.

The community consists therefore of professed monks or nuns who have already or are yet to make their solemn profession, as well as 'novices', brothers and sisters in training. This distinction establishes an order of seniority within the community and defines the place of each individual in the various areas of the monastery: the church choir, refectory, chapter, etc. [Fig. 9] Not all monks are priests; nuns never are. Besides the monks of the choir, the community includes brothers who have their own vocation and were often called 'converts' (from *conversus*, converted) or 'lay brothers'. These carry out the practical work of the abbey, in the cellar, kitchen, etc. and in the grounds. They live separately and have their own offices and customs. Certain orders, such as the Cistercians, gave lay brothers a particular role.[38] These distinctions, as well as others of social order, were relaxed and even abolished by the Second Vatican Council (1962-65) [see Chapter 14].

38 Waddell, *Cistercian Lay Brothers*.

Lastly, the members of the community carry out duties or services for fixed periods of time of varying length. Among the most important are those of the cantor, responsible for the choral liturgy, the sacristan, infirmarian, novice master, porter, guest master, librarian and archivist. They are assisted as needed by other members of the community. Some community services are reassigned on a weekly basis to allow everyone to take turns in the kitchen, at reading, in the refectory, at cleaning, etc.

These tasks are distributed and assessed together by the community in the chapter. The chapter is the daily meeting of the community in a specific room in the monastery known as the chapter room or chapter house.[39] The Rule can be found on a lectern in the middle of the room and the abbot or abbess reads and comments on a chapter every day before discussing questions of organisation and discipline. [Fig. 8] Novices take the habit and are received by the community gathered in the chapter house. In the Middle Ages, abbots and abbesses were buried there. Daily work is distributed equally in keeping with the balance required by the Rule. [Fig. 64] The monastic chapter can be regarded as one of the oldest democratic institutions in which every member of the community can express themselves with respect for others and in which decision-making has a collective dimension. The role of the abbot or abbess is decisive in maintaining the material and spiritual balance on which order in the cloister is based.

4. The Church

A place of individual or community prayer, silently or with chanting, the church is the most sacred place in the monastery. It is home to the tabernacle that contains the Blessed Sacrament, in which Catholics recognise the real presence of God, as well as an altar for the Eucharist, a cross, some holy images and benches. In an early-Christian hermitage the oratory (from *orare*, to pray) occupied a small space or a corner of the cell. As soon as there was a community, the oratory became a room in its own right, the exclusive use of which was reserved for prayer, as indicated by Saint Augustine in his monastic Rule of the late fourth century:

> Let no one do anything in the oratory except what it was built for and also takes its name from, so that, if someone wants to pray outside the appointed hours, if they have the opportunity, they should not be impeded by those who want to use the oratory for another purpose.[40]

39 Bonde, Boyden and Maines, 'Centrality and Community'; Stein-Kecks, *Der Kapitelsaal in der mittelalterlichen Klosterbaukunst.*

40 Augustin, *Œuvres complètes*, vol. 3, 587-591 (chapter 3).

Fig. 10. Cistercian abbey church of Pontigny (France), from the south-east, nave and transept from the 1140s, sanctuary from the late twelfth century.
[© Terryl N. Kinder]

The oratory was usually small in size. If the community was larger it was referred to as the chapel (*capella*, from *cappa*, cape) or church (*ecclesia*, assembly or congregation). Over the centuries, the main place of worship in an abbey or convent took a variety of different forms, scales and styles [see Chapters 19 and 21]. In all cases, its sacred function was that of the house of God within the monastery and a place of prayer for the community gathered in the name of Christ for the Eucharist and the liturgy of the hours.

From an architectural point of view, the church is undoubtedly the main building of the monastery and its location had a decisive influence on the layout of the other buildings. Christian churches are generally built along the east-west axis determined by the course of the sun. [Fig. 10] From approximately the end of the fourth century to the end of the eighth century, or rather from the Early Christian period to the Carolingian period, churches had their main entrance to the east while their sanctuary was *occidented*, in other words, facing west.[41] The main entrance of the church was often preceded by an *atrium* or courtyard surrounded by galleries, marking the transition between the church and the world, and accessible to catechumens.[42] During the Carolingian period, for liturgical reasons, the direction of churches was turned: the entrance would now be to the west and the chevet would be *oriented*, in other words, facing east. Thus the churches' axes remained the same but their direction was reversed. This norm prevailed until the nineteenth century and was

41 For example, the Basilica of Saint Peter's, built on the site of the tomb of the apostle Peter in the fourth century, was 'occidented'. The large rock basilica built in the sixteenth and seventeenth centuries on the site of the Paleochristian basilica respected this direction. For this reason its entrance is to the east and not to the west.

42 Adults following the catechism prior to their baptism.

Fig. 11. Benedictine abbey church of Stavelot (Belgium), oriented Latin cross-plan with stepped outer crypt at the east and tower at the west, eleventh century.
[© SPW-Patrimoine / photo Guy Focant]

then relaxed but not repealed. For a monastic church, orientation was an essential point. The rising of the sun after the darkness of the night was a daily reminder to the monks and nuns of the resurrection of Christ, of the triumph of life over death [see Chapter 18]. Gathered in the choir of the church for the office of lauds (*laudatio*, praises), the monks and nuns, facing east, were 'oriented towards Christ', welcoming daybreak with their chanting and giving thanks for life. [Fig. 13] Vespers (*vespera*) were the evening office.

Fig. 12. Church of Sint-Benedictusberg Abbey in Vaals (The Netherlands), designed by Dom Hans van der Laan, 1967-68; evening sun from the south-west.
[© THOC]

The orientation of the church defined two symbolic areas around which functions within the church, as well as the various zones of the abbey, were organised [see also Chapter 5]. The east was the spiritual area facing the light of the resurrection and the purity of good. It contained the most sacred functions of the church: the sanctuary, high altar, crypt and monks' choir. [Fig. 11] The west was the temporal area facing the world and sin. It contained the least sacred functions of the church: the entrance door (often associated with the Last Judgement), the lay brothers' choir, seats for guests and the seigniorial tribune. One or more towers often marked the western area of the church. Not only were these towers bell towers but their volume symbolically protected the purity of the church (east) against the evil of the world (west). The imposing westworks or *Westbau* of Carolingian churches, like large shields turned towards the world, were powerful expressions of the role of emperors or lords as protectors of the church. The Benedictine abbeys of Corvey, Nivelles, Jumièges, Tournus and Saint-Benoît-sur-Loire are spectacular examples of monastic westworks from the ninth to the eleventh centuries.[43] Many western towers are descended more or less directly from these.

Since the fourth century, large churches, including monastic churches, have taken the shape of a cross. The east-west axis of the nave and

43 Conant, *Carolingian and Romanesque Architecture*; Heitz, *L'architecture religieuse carolingienne*; Vergnolle, *Saint-Benoît-sur-Loire*, 88-94; McClendon, *The Imperial Abbey of Farfa*.

Fig. 13. The Virgin Mary presenting Jesus to Saint Dominic and his community aligned on the east-west axis of a Dominican church, circa 1500.
[© Museum Catharijneconvent, Utrecht / photo Ruben de Heer]

sanctuary is intersected by the north-south axis of the transept. [Figs 10, 11 and 18] Together this forms a cross oriented towards the four cardinal points and defines a central point at the intersection of the two axes: the crossing. The cross is described as 'Greek' when the four arms are identical in length and 'Latin' when the nave-sanctuary axis is longer than the axis of the transept.

Light moves around inside the church according to the time of day and seasonal variations in the sun's path. The religious community that gathered in the church throughout the day to chant the liturgy of the hours as set by the Rule of Saint Benedict – the full cycle consists of seven offices: matins, lauds, terce, sext, none, vespers and compline – thus experienced the cycle of light and shadows inside the sacred space on a day-to-day basis. The rays of sunlight penetrating and moving around inside the church offered a magnificent synthesis of time and the monastic space, returning in a different way each day. [Fig. 12] This daily mystical spectacle set the rhythm for the life and prayer of monks and nuns who participated by praise in the mystery of creation. Some monumental churches have a tower or dome at the crossing of the nave and transept. [Fig. 14] Lantern towers and domes add a third vertical axis to the two axes of the cross, through which zenithal or vertical light penetrates into the heart of the same space. This vertical axis, *axis mundi* or cosmic axis, is like a 'connector' linking the earth to the sky and fixing the central position of the church within the monastery. [Fig. 78]

For the monks and nuns, the physical space of the church and the liturgy experienced within it opened up their imagination to the space of another world, the paradise.[44] [Fig. 13] The physical place was the support for the abstract place of the imagination which, in turn, contributed to the sacred dimension of the physical place. This is as true of the dark crypt of a Romanesque church as of the slender choir of a Gothic church, for the powerful monumentality of Baroque churches, Rococo churches with their celestial decoration, neo-classical churches resembling ancient temples, the colourful interiors of Gothic Revival churches and the abstraction of modern churches.

Although the church is the main place of worship in a monastery, other chapels and oratories could be found in other buildings, such as the infirmary, guesthouse, abbot's lodgings and the gatehouse. These secondary oratories were intended for specific groups.

44 Cassidy-Welch, *Monastic Spaces and their Meanings*, 72-109.

Fig. 14. Benedictine abbey of Saint Riquier (France), from the south, Carolingian church built in 789-99, galleries and two chapels, engraving by Paul Petau, 1612, after a lost Carolingian drawing.

5. The Cloister

The Carolingian period played a crucial role in both the evolution of monasticism and the definition of monastic architecture. Two important events that occurred at the turn of the eighth and ninth centuries have already been mentioned: the imposition of the Rule of St Benedict on all abbeys in the Empire and the inversion of the axis of churches in an east-west direction instead of west-east. It was in this reform context that the first real cloisters began to appear, at the imperial Abbey of Lorsch in Germany, for example. Contrary to earlier periods, Carolingian architecture is known not only through excavations but also thanks to the well-preserved remains of some monuments that survive.[45]

The case of the Abbey of Saint Riquier offers a good illustration of the Carolingian policy towards abbeys. Built by Charlemagne between 789 and 799, the monumental main church, which does not survive, was designed with a dual focus: that of the community to the east (the monastic choir) and that of the emperor to the west (the westwork), each with a transept and a crossing tower.[46] [Fig. 14] An early drawing of the Abbey of Saint Riquier shows that it did not yet have a cloister in the true sense but covered walkways that linked the buildings and secondary chapels. These walkways protected the community's many movements and processions from place to place.

The large plan of an abbey kept at the Abbey of Saint Gall in Switzerland, known as the 'Plan of Saint Gall', is a remarkable document that dates from the Carolingian period, usually thought to be from the 820s.[47] The plan of an ideal abbey, it offers an extremely detailed graphic synthesis as well as written annotations about every component of an abbey. 'The plan might be fairly characterised as a two-dimensional meditation on the ideal early medieval monastic community, created at a time when monasticism was one of the dominant forms of political, economic, and cultural power in Europe.'[48] The programme is well organised and expresses an architectural understanding that is the result of both a long tradition and considerable experience. Depending on their form, the buildings were wooden and separated clearly from one another, with the exception of the church and the wings surrounding the cloister, which were built from stone. Without going into detail,

45 *Gesta. The Cloister Symposium*, 12-52; Stiegemann and Wemhoff, *799. Kunst und Kultur der Karolingerzeit*; Conant, *Carolingian and Romanesque Architecture*; Heitz, *L'architecture religieuse carolingienne*.

46 Magnien, *Saint-Riquier*.

47 This document can be consulted in detail and in context at: <http://www.stgallplan.org/>. Reference studies: Horn and Born, *The Plan of St. Gall*; Jacobsen, *Der Klosterplan von St. Gallen*; Sennhauser, *St. Gallen – Klosterplan und Gozbertbau.*

48 *Carolingian Culture at Reichenau & St. Gall. Codex Sangallensis 1092: Content and Context* <http://www.stgallplan.org/>.

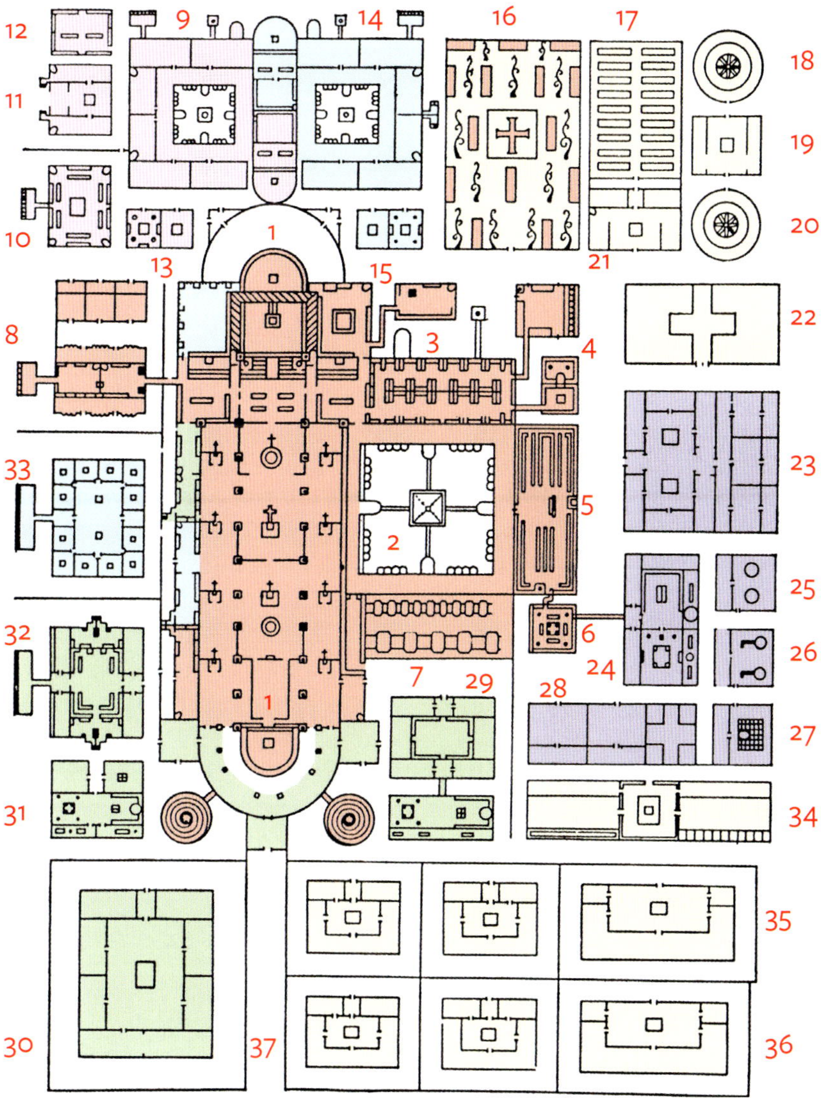

Fig. 15. Plan of Saint-Gall, Carolinian plan of an ideal abbey, 820s. 1. church, 2. cloister, 3. dormitory, 4. bath-house and latrines, 5. refectory, 6. kitchen, 7. cellar, 8. abbot's lodging and kitchen, 9. cloister for the sick and infirmary, 10. bloodletting, 11. physician, 12. medicinal garden, 13. kitchen and bath for the sick, 14. cloister for the novices and novitiate, 15. kitchen and bath for the novices, 16. monk's cemetery and orchard, 17. vegetable garden, 18. goosehouse, 19. fowlkeepers' house, 20. henhouse, 21. gardeners' house, 22. granary, 23. great collective workshop, 24. bake and brewhouse, 25. mill, 26. mortar, 27. drying kiln, 28. house of coopers and wheelwrights, and brewers' granary, 29. hospice for pilgrims and paupers, with kitchen, bake and brew house, 30. house for the emperor's vassals and knights, 31. kitchen, bake and brew house for distinguished guests, 32. house for distinguished guests, 33. outer school, 34. house for horses and oxen, 35. houses for sheep, goats and cows, 36. houses for swines, brood mares and foals, 37. house for servants of outlying estates and for the emperor's servants.
[after Lorna Price, based on Walter Horn and Ernest Born, *The Plan of St Gall in Brief*, 1982]

church, monastic buildings · education · crafts and milling
health, medicine · agriculture · reception

the functions of the buildings can be grouped into six different areas around the cloister, in accordance with the symbolic orientation [Fig. 15]: 1. the church to the north of the cloister and the community buildings around the cloister; 2. buildings for novices and the infirm around two small cloisters to the east of the church choir; 3. the cemetery, farmyard and kitchen garden to the north east; 4. the industrial buildings, including a mill, forge, bakery and a brewery to the south, close to a water course by necessity; 5. the agricultural buildings, grange and stables to the south east; 6. buildings in which to accommodate guests to the west. These six zones had distinct functions and, as a result, were not accessible to the same groups of people.

A square cloister with rounded arches marks the centre of the monastic Plan of Saint Gall. The cloister was one of the Carolingian reform's most significant contributions to monastic architecture. Its role is functional and its meaning symbolic. At the centre of the abbey, it forms a square courtyard surrounded by galleries that links the church and various monastic spaces, notably the refectory, chapter house and dormitory, in a rational and organised manner. The church usually occupies the northern flank of the cloister. If the east-west orientation of the church is spiritual and symbolic, its location north of the cloister is purely functional. Its height protects the cloister from cold winds but it does not cast its shadow over the cloister. In the warm regions of Southern Europe it is not unusual for a church to be to the south of the cloister; in these cases its shadow falls on the cloister, keeping it cool.[49] Reserved for monks and nuns only, the cloister should not be confused with the *atrium*, which existed since the fourth century and could be found in front of the main façade of churches.[50]

The cloister is therefore enclosed, as its name would indicate: *claustrum* meaning 'enclosure' or 'barrier'. Its only opening is vertical, towards the sky. Such was the perspective of the monk, who lived on earth and aspired to the afterlife. The medieval abbey was therefore designed and experienced as a quest for perfection in the chaos of the world, and took as its reference the New Jerusalem, the vision of which is described in the Apocalypse.[51] The 'New Jerusalem' or 'Heavenly Jerusalem', the holy city of God, is a traditional Jewish and Christian concept, associated simultaneously with paradise, the Promised Land and the rebuilding of the Temple of Jerusalem after the Jewish captivity in Babylon. According to tradition, the New Jerusalem could be a literal city or a spiritual and mystical place, even embodying the return to the

49 *Carolingian Culture at Reichenau & St. Gall.*

50 The *atrium* disappeared roughly between the eighth and eleventh centuries. It survives in rare cases in monastic churches, such as at Maria Laach.

51 *Gesta. The Cloister Symposium*, 53-69; Meyer, *Medieval Allegory and the Building of the New Jerusalem.*

Fig. 16. Double storied cloister and fountain house at the Royal Monastery of Santa Mariá of Guadalupe (Spain), built circa 1400.
[© THOC]

perfection of the original paradise. Thus the material space of the cloister was experienced as a metaphorical space symbolising paradise.[52] The symbolism of the enclosed garden (*hortus conclusus*) had a particular mystical significance for communities of nuns and Beguines.[53]

In the centre or in a corner of the cloister near the refectory is a functioning fountain symbolising the presence of Christ, source of the water of life. [Fig. 16] Before entering the refectory, the monks would wash their face and hands in this fountain, also known as the *lavatorium*. This simple gesture of physical hygiene also had a spiritual dimension as it referred to rituals of purification before eating, particularly to the washing of the apostles' feet by Christ before the Last Supper. Once a week, usually on Saturday mornings, the abbot, like Christ, would wash the feet of members of the community. This ritual, known as the *mandatum*, would take place in the cloister gallery that ran along the church.

52 Cassidy-Welch, *Monastic Spaces and their Meanings*, 47-71; Sennhauser, *St. Gallen – Klosterplan und Gozbertbau*, 33-50.

53 Vandenbroeck, *Le jardin clos de l'âme.*

Fig. 17. Franciscan brothers in the cloister of the monastery of Santa Maria in Ara Coeli, Rome (Italy), romantic painting by Judocus Sebastiaen Van den Abeele, 1842.
[© Musée de l'Oise, Beauvais / photo RMN-Grand Palais, Adrien Didierjean]

At the centre of daily life for the monks and nuns, the cloister was both material and spiritual. [Fig. 17] The medieval cloister was a versatile place:

> Ultimately the cloister was the multi-purpose place for the monastic community. A place through which to pass but also in which to stay, for silent reading at certain times of the day or to talk at other times; a place that was home to many of the small jobs of daily life; where mutual services were rendered, such as shaving or washing feet. Yet it was also a place where the atmosphere of liturgical ritual, the backdrop of medieval monastic life, always came first, while liturgical solemnity was freely deployed there during the many processions.[54]

54 Davril, 'Fonctions des cloîtres'.

After the Middle Ages, the cloister lost this versatility and became above all a place of silence and passage. In particular, it lost its role as a place of reading (*lectio divina*) as the manuscripts that were kept in the cloister's niches or cupboards (*armarium*) were moved into libraries. The considerable increase in books following the invention of printing led to the building of libraries.

Historically, the cloister remained a central place within the monastic or conventual enclosure, protected and turned inwards around an enclosed garden with a perspective of heavenly perfection. For this reason, cloisters were the focus of attention from their occupants in search of the absolute: whether Romanesque, Gothic, Baroque, neo-Gothic or modern, cloisters sometimes decorated, sometimes simple, were always open to the light, depending on the proportions, rhythms and plays of immense creativity.[55] Some decorations deemed excessive gave rise to criticism.[56]

Like the square cloister, defined during the Carolingian period, the monastery was a rigid institution, subject to a rule. However, a space of freedom existed within this framework that allowed the individual to develop spiritually. This is without a doubt the main key for those who want to understand the order around the cloister.

55 Klein, *Der mittelalterliche Kreuzgang*.
56 About Saint Bernard's critics in the *Apology to William of St. Thierry*, 1125, see Chapter 20.

Fig. 18. Ruins of the Cistercian abbey of Villers (Belgium), from the south-west, thirteenth to eighteenth centuries.
[© SPW-Patrimoine / photo Guy Focant]

BUILDING TYPES

IDENTITIES AND REFORMATIONS

After establishing the origin and meaning of the cell, church and cloister, the three essential elements of monastic life in the Western Christian tradition, we now need to consider the various architectural types. How, in essence, did monastic architecture respond to the identity of specific 'religious families' according to different rules and apostolates, in other words to their individual identities?

There is a wide range of religious orders and institutes, male and female, contemplative, mendicant, military, hospitaller, teaching, missionary, etc. [Figs 2-3] These have appeared and developed over the centuries in response to the precise needs of society at given moments in history. Many male and female religious orders and institutes disappeared because they were unable to adapt to the evolution of society, either being abolished violently or failing to recruit and dying slowly. The ability to reform, that is to adapt the monastic tradition to changes in society, without losing their specific identity, has always been a major challenge for religious orders and institutes. Some reformed from within, others split into distinct branches or even into new orders. The Cistercians, for example, were founded in 1098 following a reform of Benedictine abbeys, but were divided in turn in the seventeenth century into 'Cistercians of Common Observance' and 'Cistercians of Strict Observance', also known as Trappists, whose destinies evolved in parallel after the French Revolution.[57] Without a doubt, the 'Franciscan family' offered the most complex range of different branches and 'distant cousins' who shared the Rule of

57 Pacaut, *Les moines blancs.*

Saint Francis like a common DNA.[58] Conversely, the Franciscan mosaic contrasted with the solid centralised structure of the Society of Jesus.[59] With the emergence of national identities since the fifteenth century, religious orders were structured into networks, then into increasingly autonomous national congregations. Alongside these international networks, many local congregations, linked to a particular project in a diocese or country, had a limited lifespan. Others, whose vocations dried up in their countries of origin, underwent new developments in mission countries and went on to become autonomous. Whatever the case, the history of religious orders and institutes is inseparable from that of individuals, monks and nuns, founders and reformers, contemplatives and actives, intellectuals and manual workers, saints and anonymous figures...

This great diversity of Christian religious communities has generated countless monasteries, abbeys, convents and other religious houses. Nine architectural types are addressed here and related to specific religious orders and apostolates: the abbey, charterhouse, castle or commandry, mendicant friary, beguinage, Hôtel-Dieu or hospital, college, palace and house monastery.

6. The Abbey

The type of the abbey concerns the great monastic and canonical families, of both men and women: the Benedictines and the Augustinian Canons Regular, as well as the reforming orders founded within them in the late eleventh century, the Cistercians and the Premonstratensians in particular. These religious orders built thousands of abbeys, the scale and style of which varied. Their basic layout remained close to the principles set down in the Plan of Saint Gall, however. [Fig. 15]

After the Carolingian period, Europe suffered the Norman and Hungarian invasions, which caused the ruin of many abbeys. A renewal began in the monastic world in the tenth century, under the impetus of the Benedictine Abbey of Cluny in Burgundy. Founded in 910, Cluny was transformed in less than two centuries into a veritable capital of a spiritual and temporal 'Cluniac' empire that included over 1,500 abbeys and priories across Europe.[60] Its influence was considerable, not just from a spiritual point of view but also from a political, economic, architectural and artistic one (music, illumination, sculpture, goldsmithing, etc.). The architecture of many Benedictine abbey churches of the eleventh and twelfth centuries, with their powerful volumes punctuated by towers, affirmed not only their spiritual influences but also their temporal

58 Vorreux, 'Les Franciscains'.

59 Rideau, 'Saint Ignace et la Compagnie de Jésus'.

60 Mullins, *Cluny*; Pacaut, *L'Ordre de Cluny*; Evans, *Monastic Life at Cluny*; Stratford et al., *Cluny 910-2010*; Hurel and Riche, *Cluny*.

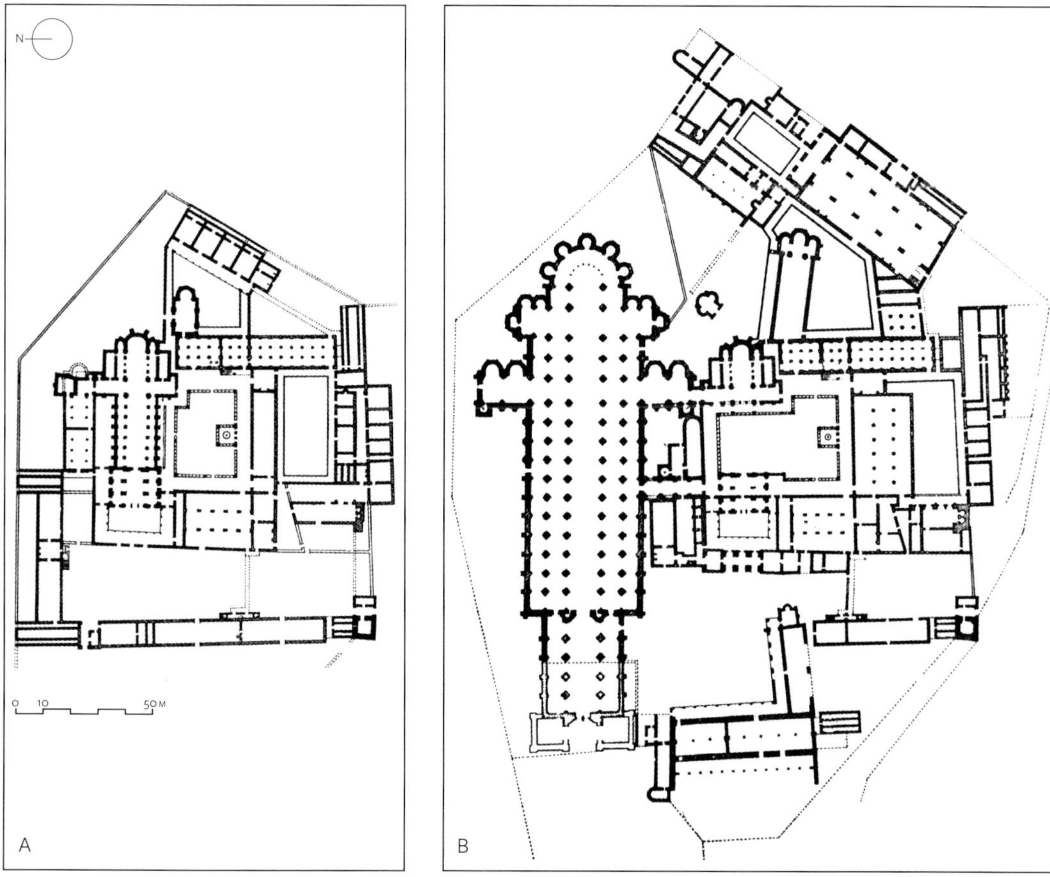

Fig. 19. Benedictine abbey of Cluny (France): A. eleventh-century abbey (Cluny II); B. twelfth-century abbey (Cluny III), plans on the same scale. [From: K.J. Conant, *Cluny*, 1968]

and political power over important feudal domains (Saint-Benoît-sur-Loire, Fontgombault, Caen, Maria Laach, Cuxa, Paray-le-Monial, Tournus, Conques, etc.).[61] Destroyed during the French Revolution, few medieval buildings at the Abbey of Cluny survive, but archaeological studies have made it possible to reconstruct its plan and evolution.[62]

A comparison, on the same scale, of the two main phases of the abbey speaks at length for itself. [Fig. 19] Cluny II was its state in the mid-eleventh century, and Cluny III, a century later, came after the completion of the new church. With a length of 187 metres, it was the largest in Christendom. Despite the size of the abbey, the layout around the cloister remained faithful to the tradition set in place during the Carolingian period. The growth of the abbey

61 Krüger, *Die romanischen Westbauten*.

62 Baud, *Cluny*; Conant, *Cluny*.

involved ingenious solutions and applied the principle of centrifugal growth [see Chapter 19]: the cloister remained the generating element and the peripheral buildings developed centrifugally in all directions, taking topography into account and separating specific functional zones. The church occupied the north side of the cloister and was preceded, to the west, by an atrium; the monks' wing with the chapter house, parlour, workroom and dormitories upstairs formed the east side; the south side consisted of the warming house and the refectory; the kitchen and the cellar closed off the cloister to the west. As in the Plan of Saint Gall, according to symbolic orientation, buildings developed beyond the cloister and were linked by galleries to its peripheral buildings. The infirmary buildings and herbs garden were further to the east of the monks' wing. In the extension of this to the south, latrines and bathhouses preceded the novitiate. Workshops, as well as the bakery, adjoined to the kitchen, were located around a large courtyard to the south of the refectory. Finally, to the west of the church and the cellar, around a large courtyard, came the buildings which, by their function, were the most focused on the world at large: the guesthouse, stables, an almshouse or chaplaincy and the gatehouse. The plan of Cluny III revealed a significant change in scale [see Chapter 19], but the distribution of functions and general morphology remained roughly identical. At its centre, however, the cloister was extended to encompass the nave of the church of Cluny II, while the new church, instead of being superimposed over the old one, developed beyond it. [Fig. 19]

In the eleventh century, the popes implemented new reforms aimed at steadying the ship of the Church; these were known as the 'Gregorian reform', initiated by Gregory VII († 1085), a pope of monastic origin.[63] This reform had three objectives: firstly, the affirmation of the independence of the clergy in relation to political power, in particular for appointments; secondly, the reform of the clergy by the affirmation of their celibacy and the improvement of their level of training; thirdly, the affirmation of the role of the pope and the development of a centralised administration. The Gregorian reform had profound consequences for the monastic world because the Benedictine model, dominant since the Carolingian period, was challenged from the inside by reforming monks and abbots, some of whom did not hesitate to dissent and found new orders with the objective of living in accordance with a stricter application of the Rule. Among the many reforms, the most spectacular was that of the Abbey of Cîteaux, founded in 1098 in Burgundy, which gave rise to the Cistercian order and found itself at the head of an organised network of more than 1,200 abbeys in less than a century and a half.[64] Although he was not the founder of the order, Saint Bernard of Clairvaux († 1153) was the most

63 Gouguenheim, *La réforme grégorienne*; Laudage, *Gregorianische Reform und Investiturstreit*.

64 Lekai, *The Cistercians*; Pacaut, *Les moines blancs*; Van der Meer, *Atlas de l'ordre cistercien*.

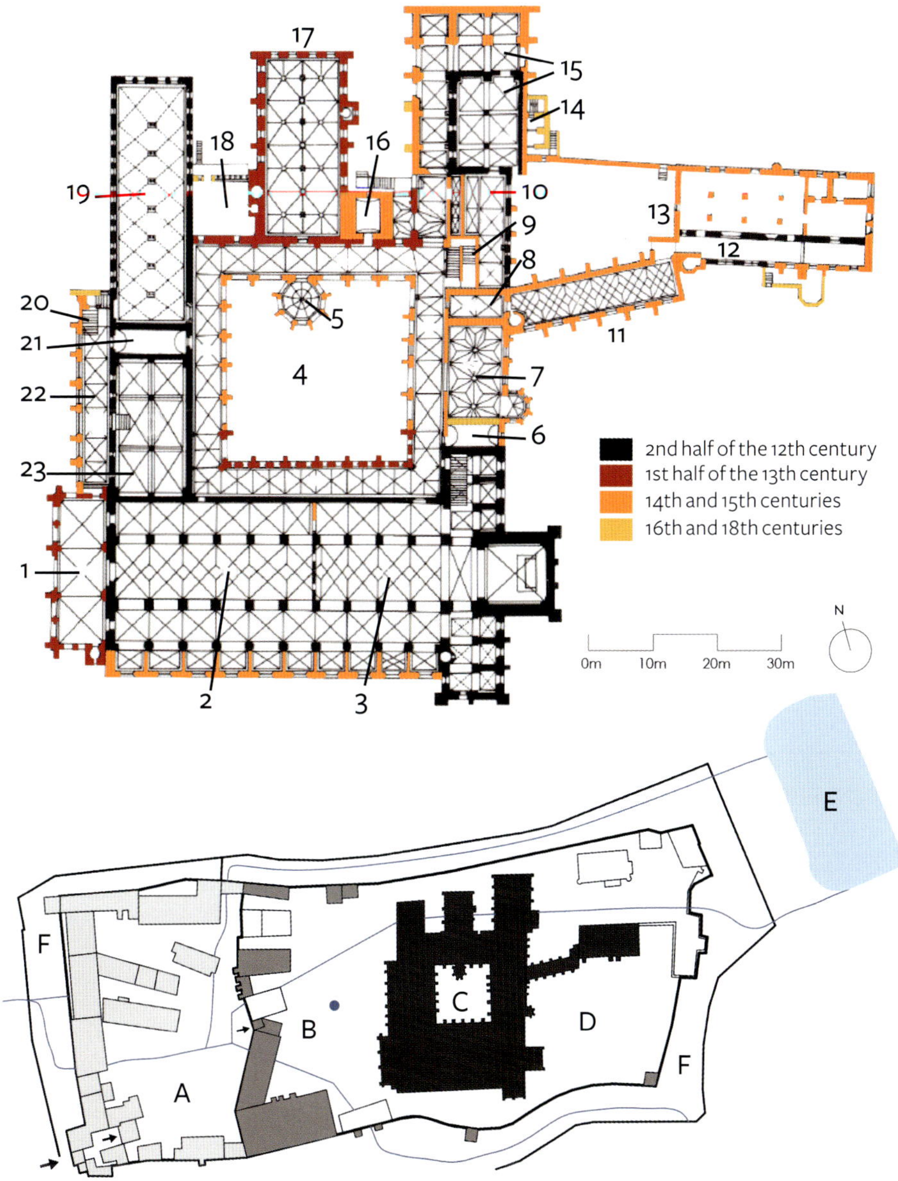

Fig. 20. Cistercian abbey of Maulbronn (Germany), plans of the monastic buildings and the whole abbey.
1. porch, 2. lay brothers' church, 3. monks' church, 4. cloister, 5. fountain, 6. sacristy, 7. chapter house, 8. passageway, 9. stairs to the monks' dormitory, 10. monks' common room, library, 11. parlour and chapel above, 12. infirmary, 13. abbot's room, 14. latrines, 15. undercroft, storeroom, 16. warming room, 17. monks' refectory, 18. kitchen, 19. lay brothers' refectory, 20. stairs to the lay brothers' dormitory, 21. passageway, 22. lay brothers' cloister gallery, 23. cellar.
A. outer court (gatehouse, guest house, mill, ancillary buildings), B. inner court (bursar's office, lay brothers' workshops, storage, barn), C. church and monastic buildings (detailed above), D. cemetery, E. fish pond and water system (blue), F. precinct wall and towers.
[After Peter Anstett, *Kloster Maulbronn*]

Fig. 21. Dormitory of the Cistercian abbey of Alcobaça (Portugal), thirteenth century. [© THOC]

remarkable Cistercian and was known as a 'theologian of monastic life'.[65] [Figs 4 and 8].

In their quest for purity and reform, the Cistercians of the twelfth century systematised the plan of their abbeys to the extent that some historians have mistakenly spoken of a 'typical plan'.[66] Rather, it was a question of the strict application of the monastic tradition and the organisation of time and space. The morphology of the abbey was the result of a rigorous programme, but one that nevertheless adapted to the topography of the site and the size of the community. [Fig. 20] The notion of Cistercian art and architecture is derived more from a spirit, a sense of proportions and a decorative simplicity than the morphology of the abbey itself.[67] The order around the Cistercian cloister was the culmination of centuries of experience; in its compactness and functionality, it was close to perfection and was supposed to lead to perfection. The main difference when compared to a Benedictine abbey concerned the west wing of the cloister, intended for Cistercian lay brothers. The lay brothers had a distinct vocation from that of the monks; they took care of service in the abbey and on its grounds, lived in distinct buildings and had their own liturgy in the church.

65 In the plentiful literature, in particular: Leclercq, *Bernard of Clairvaux*; Pressouyre and Kinder, eds, *Saint Bernard*; Kinder and Cassanelli, eds, *The Cistercian Arts*.

66 Coomans, 'Cistercian Architecture or Architecture of the Cistercians?'. The idea of a 'typical plan' was the fruit of the rationalist spirit of the nineteenth century, but a medieval abbey was obviously not like a station, school or standardised barracks.

67 Kinder, *Cistercian Europe*; Untermann, *Forma ordinis*.

Fig. 22. Refectory of the Trappist abbey of La Grande-Trappe (France), built by Alfred Tessier in 1887. [Postcard, circa 1900 , private collection]

Besides the abbey church, facing east and usually to the north of the cloister [see Chapter 4], the morphology of a Cistercian abbey included the following components.[68] [Fig. 20] In the middle of the east wing, the chapter house was a centrally planned room with a vaulted ceiling in which the community would gather daily under the direction of the abbot. The monks would sit on benches arranged along the walls, while a lectern bearing the Rule could be found in the middle of the room.[69] [Fig. 8] The upstairs of the east wing was occupied by a large shared dormitory, either vaulted or with beams, accessible by two staircases: one leading to the cloister, the other directly to the church for night-time offices. [Fig. 21] It was not until the end of the thirteenth century, with the advent of a concern for privacy, that the dormitories were divided into alcoves. From the sixteenth century onwards these became proper rooms.

The wing of the cloister that was parallel to the church was dominated by the refectory in which the monks would gather twice a day after cleaning themselves in the cloister fountain. The tables were arranged parallel to the walls and the vegetarian meal was taken in silence. [Fig. 22] The size of the refectories was explained by their symbolic dimension as the shared meal commemorated the Last Supper taken by Christ and the apostles. To the east

68 Amongst others: Aubert and de Maillé, *L'architecture cistercienne en France*; Coppack, *The White Monks*; Kinder, *Cistercian Europe*; Robinson, *The Cistercian Abbeys of Britain*. Abbey monographs include: Fergusson and Harrison, *Rievaulx Abbey*; Coomans, *L'abbaye de Villers-en-Brabant*.

69 Bonde, Boyden and Maines, 'Centrality and Community'.

Fig. 23. Cistercian abbey of Rievaulx (England): infirmary hall from 1155-57, converted to the abbot's residence circa 1500.
[© THOC]

of the refectory was the chauffoir, the only room with an open fire accessible to the monks. To the west of the refectory was the kitchen, which also served the refectory of the lay brothers, who occupied the west wing of the abbey, symbolically facing the world and the grounds. The lay brothers were therefore completely separated from the monks and had their own courtyard, the 'lay brothers' lane', which led to the area of the church reserved for them. Their buildings included a refectory, dormitory, infirmary, latrines, etc. [Fig. 20] With the disappearance of lay brothers during the thirteenth century, their buildings were reassigned or destroyed.

Beyond the cloister, as in the Plan of Saint Gall, the novitiate, infirmary and cemetery were situated to the east, while the guesthouse, gatehouse, workshops and the domestic farm extended towards the west. [Figs 20, 23 and 24] Inside the enclosure, not all these buildings were accessible to everyone and were governed by a different enclosure we will examine further on [see Chapter 16]. Finally, the abbey grounds, including woods, fields, pastures, fish ponds, vineyards, mines, etc. were operated and managed by large farms known as 'granges'.[70]

70 Pressouyre, *L'espace cistercien*.

Fig. 24. Gatehouse of the Premonstratensian abbey of Tongerlo (Belgium), sixteenth century. [© THOC]

The building sites of abbeys in keeping with the basic plan described here could be found in their thousands across Europe during the eleventh and twelfth centuries. Some remarkable fragments survive, much to the delight of enthusiasts of Romanesque art and architecture. Over the following centuries, the majority of abbeys were transformed in turn without any fundamental questioning of a layout that was adequate and formed part of tradition. A sixteenth- or eighteenth-century Benedictine abbey, despite the reforms and its very different external appearance – notably, the style of its buildings [see Chapter 20], as well as their comfort and the layout of its garden – more or less reproduced the outline of a twelfth-century abbey following the Plan of Saint Gall. Improvements in comfort consisted in particular of an improvement in heating through the increase in the number of fireplaces, the glazing of cloister galleries and greater privacy provided by the replacement of shared dormitories by individual rooms, etc.

The literature on monastic architecture gives pride of place to medieval Benedictine and Cistercian abbeys. In England, ten abbeys were uniquely also cathedrals and their abbots therefore also bishops. The remarkable architecture, scale and famous polygonal chapter houses of these 'cathedral

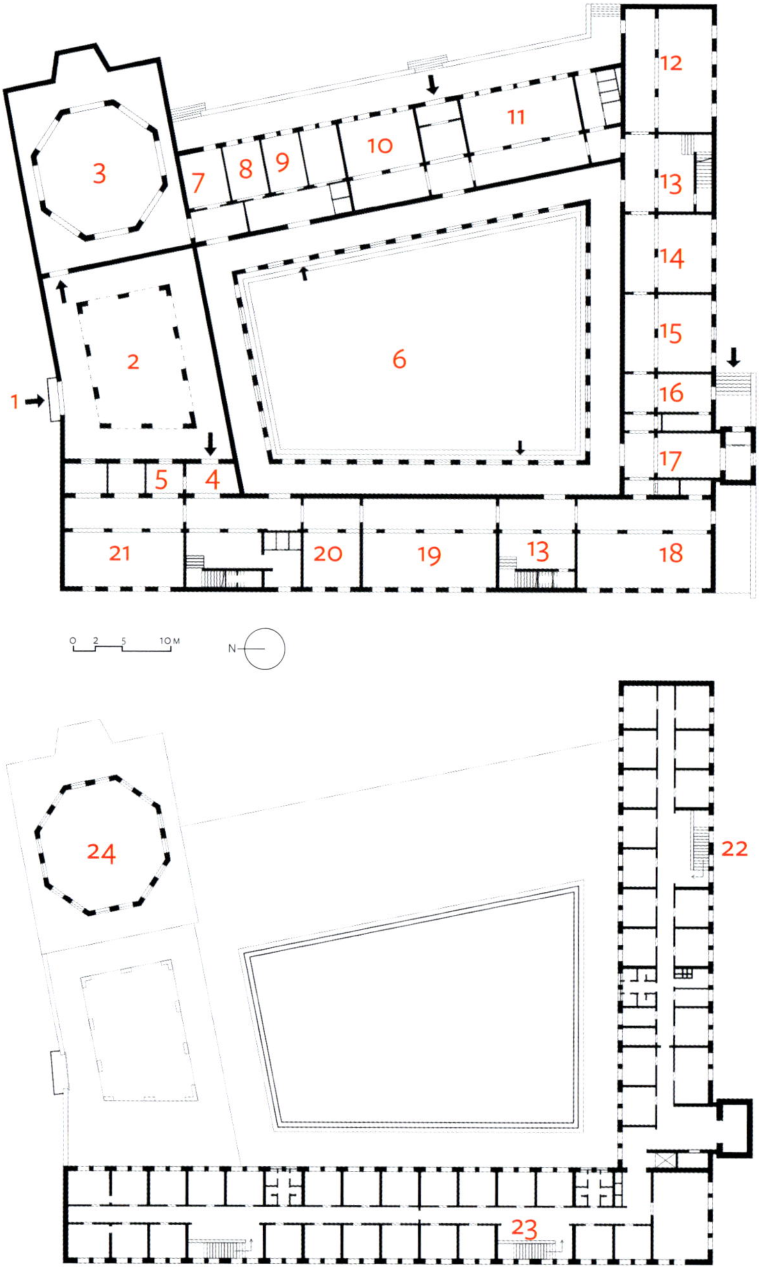

Fig. 25. Franciscan convent of Roosenberg in Waasmunster (Belgium), 1971, by Dom Hans van der Laan: 1. entrance, 2. forecourt or atrium, 3. church, 4. entrance to the convent, 5. porter's lodge, 6. cloister, 7. sacristy, 8. parlour, 9. office, 10. study room, 11. work room, 12. recreation room, 13. staircase, 14. refectory, 15. kitchen, 16. dishes, 17. hall of the back entrance, 18. guests' refectory, 19. conference room, 20. reception room, 21. museum. Upper floor: 22. wing with the nuns' cells, 23. guests' rooms, 24. church's clerestorey. [© Caroline Voet]

monasteries' have been subject to detailed study.[71] There has been a genuine 'historiographical injustice' with regard to other monastic orders and periods. This is particularly because of the numerical importance of Benedictine and Cistercian abbeys, the remarkable quality of numerous Romanesque and Gothic abbeys, as well as the many ruins, some of which are majestic.[72] Other canonical or monastic orders resulting from the Gregorian reform, such as the Premonstratensians or Norbertines, the order of Arrouaise, the order of Fontevrault, the order of Grandmont, the congregation of Victorines and the order of Trinitaires have not benefited from the same interest from architectural historians, archeologists or tourism networks.

The architecture of later periods, from the late Middle Ages to the twentieth century, with a few exceptions – in particular the 'palace' type [see Chapter 13] – has been largely ignored. The same goes for the revival of monastic architecture in the nineteenth century, which referred often explicitly to the medieval model of the 'abbey' type as well as to medieval styles.[73] [Figs 22, 78 and 80] The abbey type with its central cloister and east-west orientation was questioned in the context of the Second Vatican Council (1962-65) by several communities who experienced other designs such as the 'house monastery' [see chapters 14 and 20]. At the same time, however, other communities built new abbeys in the modern style but retained the traditional plan. This is true of the Abbey of Roosenberg in Waasmunster, designed in 1971 by the Benedictine monk-architect Hans van der Laan († 1991) for a community of Franciscan sisters.[74] Despite the trapezoidal plan of the cloister and central plan of the church, Van der Laan's rigorous proportion system serves a traditional enlaced spatial organisation, with clearly distinct areas and circulations between the nuns' enclosure and the guest wing. [Fig. 25]

7. The Charterhouse

A second architectural type is that of the charterhouse, which appeared at the end of the eleventh century against the backdrop of Gregorian reform. In 1084, Saint Bruno († 1101) founded a hermitage in the Grande Chartreuse mountains near Grenoble. [Fig. 26] This was the starting point for a new and purely

71 The cathedrals of Canterbury, Bath, Durham, Ely, Norwich, Rochester, Winchester, Worcester, Coventry and Carlisle. After the Anglican reform, the cathedrals were maintained and these abbeys became secular chapters; their heritage remained intact. Braunfels, *Monasteries of Western Europe*, 153-174.

72 Among the most remarkable: Fountains, Rievaulx, Glastonbury, Kirkstall, Byland (England), Melrose (Scotland), Jumièges (France), Villers (Belgium), Moreruela (Spain), San Galgano (Italy), Hirsau and Heisterbach (Germany), etc. [see Chapter 21].

73 Brittain-Catlin, De Maeyer and Bressani, eds, *Gothic Revival Worldwide*; Young, 'A.W.N. Pugin's Mount Saint Bernard Abbey'.

74 Voet, *Dom Hans van der Laan*.

Fig. 26. Monastery of La Grande Chartreuse (France), head monastery of the Carthusian order, founded in 1084 in the Alps.
[© Hemis/Alamy Stock Photo]

contemplative order that combined extreme eremitism with the demands of religious life in a community.[75] There are currently twenty-five charterhouses around the world, including six for women. The documentary film *Into Great Silence* is a gripping account of daily life at La Grande Chartreuse.[76]

Carthusian architecture was original and expressed the order's way of life, a sort of community eremitism or 'communities of silence'. In isolated locations, the monks lived in complete solitude in hermitage houses arranged around a cloister. In principle, a Carthusian community consists of twelve monks and a prior, but some communities have several dozen monks. [Fig. 69] They only leave their cells three times a day, for mass and community prayers in the church. Once a week, on Sundays, they gather in the chapter house and eat together in the refectory.

The cells are like small houses or hermitages with three rooms, a fireplace, sometimes an upstairs and a fenced garden with a latrine at the bottom. The Carthusians have a few pieces of furniture and some basic tools at their disposal. They pray, sleep, read, eat and work in their cell. Next to the door is a hatch through which meals are delivered by a lay brother. The cells are arranged around three sides of the cloister, the central space of which also serves as a cemetery. [Figs 27 and 69] The church, generally small and with a single nave, occupies the fourth side, with the chapterhouse, the refectory, the library and the prior's cell. In a charterhouse, the notion of order around the cloister reaches its culmination. In front of the church is a service courtyard with the gatehouse and logistical buildings.[77]

75 Lockhart, *Halfway to Heaven*; Le Bras, 'Les Chartreux'.
76 *Die große Stille*, by Philip Gröning, 2005.
77 Coppack and Aston, *Christ's Poor Men*; Braunfels, *Monasteries of Western Europe*, 111-124.

Fig. 27. Carthusian hermitage houses around the Grand Cloister of the Certosa di Pavia (Italy), second half of the fifteenth century.
[© THOC]

In the late Middle Ages, charterhouses were founded near towns by sovereigns who richly endowed them and were buried within them. As a result, the charterhouses of Villeneuve-les-Avignon,[78] Champmol in Dijon, Miraflores in Burgos, and Certosa di Pavia – endowed respectively by the popes, the dukes of Burgundy, the kings of Castile and the Visconti of Milan – contrasted by their sumptuousness with the Carthusian ideal without affecting the austerity and essence of the lives of the monks. Many charterhouses were demolished in the late eighteenth century, but some were converted and can be visited.

Other religious orders attracted by the eremitic lifestyle adopted the charterhouse type as an architectural model. The Camaldolese, founded by Saint Romuald († 1027) in the context of the Gregorian reform, developed an original contemplative lifestyle combining eremitism and monasticism: the hermits lived in cells comparable to those of the Carthusians, while the monks lived in monasteries. In Camaldoli in Tuscany the two establishments, separated by three kilometres, share the same site. The hermitages are small houses with enclosed gardens. They are not arranged around the cloister but in a chequerboard fashion inside a large space surrounded by a wall. Other active urban orders, such as the Discalced Carmelites, owned 'holy deserts' in the countryside that the brothers would visit at regular intervals for spells of healing and meditation. These 'deserts' could be found in remote places and resembled charterhouses.

78 Sournia and Vayssettes, *Villeneuve-lès-Avignon*, 197-227 and 293-318.

Fig. 28. Cloister and round church of the Convent of Christ in Tomar (Portugal), originally of the Knights Templars, replaced by the Knights of the Order of Christ from 1312.
[© Hans Blossey / Alamy Stock Photo]

8. The Castle

Military orders were the contemporaries of the Carthusians and Cistercians but were radically different. These groups of knights lived in communities in accordance with the canonical rule and respected the vows of poverty, chastity and obedience. Military orders were founded in the twelfth century in the context of the armed struggle against the Muslims, during the Crusades in the Holy Land and the *reconquista* in Spain and Portugal.[79] The initial vocation of these orders was to provide security and accommodate pilgrims visiting Palestine after the conquest of Jerusalem in 1099. The aim of these 'soldiers of Christ' (*milites Christi*) was to 'lead a religious life while exercising the profession of arms', something that seems completely irreconcilable today. The major orders of the Holy Land were the order of the Temple or the Knights Templars, the order of the Knights of the Hospital of Saint John of Jerusalem, the Knights of the Holy Sepulchre and the Teutonic Knights. The military orders of the *reconquista* were the orders of Alcántara, Avis, Calatrava, Christ, Santiago, etc. The organisation of these orders was complicated: they included companies dependent on 'commanders' and subject to a 'grand master'. A certain degree of flexibility forced them to adapt continually to contexts of war and sometimes significant losses of men.

The monasteries of these military orders were called commandries and looked less to abbeys and more to fortified castles or barracks. In conflict

79 Demurger, *Chevaliers du Christ*; Cocheril, 'Les ordres militaires et hospitaliers'; Novoa Portela and De Ayala Martínez, eds, *Las Órdines Militares en la Europa Medieval*.

Fig. 29. Malbork Castle of the Teutonic Knights (Poland), thirteenth century.
[© Mauritius images / Alamy Stock Photo]

zones, their buildings were fortresses, the most famous of which was the Krak des Chevaliers in Syria, reputed to be impregnable but which capitulated in 1271. The castle-monastery of Calatrava in Castile also demonstrated that these citadels lost their *raison d'être* and were abandoned once the conflict had ended or moved on. Military orders also had landholdings outside the combat territories, originating from donations intended to provide them with income, just like the granges of abbey estates. When not in conflict zones, commandries were large fortified farms that included a chapel and all the buildings necessary for the lives of the inhabitants: housing, refectory, stables, chapter house, etc.

After the loss of the Holy Land in 1291, military orders had to refocus their activities in Europe. The case of the Knights Templars, suppressed by the King of France and the pope in 1312, was much written about and bordered on myth.[80] Their architecture was recognisable from their centrally planned churches that referred to the Temple of Jerusalem, or more exactly to the Dome of the Rock on the temple esplanade. [Fig. 28] In Paris, the church of the Templars combined a 'rotunda' and a very elongated monastic choir; in the thirteenth century, they erected a large tower about 50 m high, a symbol of their military and political power.

German knights had founded a military order in the Holy Land that also established commandries in Central Europe.[81] When the Crusaders lost the Holy Land, these Teutonic knights founded a theocratic state in East Prussia –

80 Amongst others: Sean, *The Knights Templar*; Demurger, *Les Templiers*.
81 Buschinger and Mathieu, *Les Chevaliers teutoniques*; Sonthofen, *Der Deutsche Orden*.

the Monastic State of the Teutonic Knights – and led a crusade against the kings of Poland. This state existed until the early sixteenth century and had as its capital the formidable fortress of Marienburg, now Malbork, on the Vistula. [Fig. 29] This Gothic and brick-built architectural complex consisted of three castles intertwined and separated by ditches and enclosures: firstly, the upper castle or fortified monastery with chapel, cloister and armoury; secondly, the middle castle or palace of the grand master of the order, with a large courtyard and service wings, including large stables; thirdly, the lower section, which was home to the merchants.

The military orders that survived the Middle Ages were transformed into secular chivalric orders, under the authority of a sovereign, such as the present sovereign and military order of Malta, descended from the Knights of the Hospital of Saint John of Jerusalem.

9. The Friary

In the thirteenth century, the Church was forced once again to adapt to an evolving society. The development of towns gave rise to a new urban society, consisting of new bourgeois, working-class and poor social classes. The centres of gravity of feudal, rural and agricultural societies moved towards towns and a new economy based on trade, industry and crafts. From a religious perspective, towns, places of greater freedom and contestation, saw the development of new religious movements for both men and women, some of which did not conform to the doctrines of the Church. The Church was therefore faced with heresies, including, most significantly, those of the Cathars and the Vaudois,[82] as well as scourges that developed on the margins of urban society, such as poverty, epidemics, prostitution, etc. The former diocesan and parochial structures, as well as rural abbeys, were not able to develop an appropriate apostolate.

The movement of the mendicant orders was spontaneous and extremely diversified, in turn becoming a threat to the established Church.[83] Groups of brothers, who depended on begging to live, began preaching in the towns, and groups of men and women gathered to help in the hospitals and leprosaria. Most claimed apostolic poverty and criticised the authorities, wealth and power. The emblematic figure of this movement was Saint Francis of Assisi († 1226), father of the Order of the Friars Minor and the Franciscan family, and author of a rule of life that bears his name.[84] Saint Elizabeth of Hungary († 1231), from the Third Order of Saint Francis, dedicated herself to the poor

82 Lambert, *Medieval Heresy*.

83 Lawrence, *The Friars*.

84 Amongst others: Le Goff, *Saint Francis of Assisi*; Thompson, *Francis of Assisi*; Vauchez, *Francis of Assisi*, as well as the film *Brother Sun, Sister Moon*, by Franco Zeffirelli, 1972.

and sick. Saint Dominic of Guzman († 1221) founded the Order of Friars Preachers or Dominicans, who fought heresies through preaching and inquisition. In 1274, the Holy See officially recognised four 'mendicant orders': the Franciscans, Dominicans, Carmelites and Hermits of Saint Augustine.[85] The other spontaneous movements were condemned to disappear.

Every town in the Western world would possess at least one mendicant friary and nunnery, but in large towns and more urbanised regions – Northern Italy and the Southern Low Countries – all four orders had a presence. The ideal of poverty prevented them from owning landed property and living off income in the way traditional abbeys did. They had to live off alms thanks to preaching, confession and the overseeing of burials that formed the essence of their ministry. Through study and links with the academic world in the towns of the thirteenth century, the mendicant orders mastered the theology that allowed them to fight heresy. In *The Name of the Rose*, Umberto Eco pits a Dominican against a Franciscan leading the inquisition in a Benedictine abbey.[86]

The mendicant orders lived in towns and the immediate periphery of growing towns, in monasteries whose morphology was adapted to the land available [see Chapter 15]. Unlike the abbey, the mendicant friary developed a flexible and dynamic architecture, resembling permanent building sites and enlarging churches and cloisters to welcome more tombs and provide preaching. After several centuries of acquisitions and extensions, mendicant friaries owned entire urban blocks and their buildings were often in contradiction with their original ideals of poverty. [Fig. 30]

Like the abbey, the mendicant friary developed around a rectangular cloister, but in a way that was often more irregular. The mendicant church consisted of two sections: a choir for the offices and a hall-nave for preaching and burials.[87] The poverty of the architecture was expressed through the absence of towers, transepts and architectural decoration, which did not exclude monumentality. These churches were like large empty boxes that were gradually filled with sumptuous gifts, private chapels from patrician families, corporations and brotherhoods.

A sacristy, chapter house, refectory, kitchen and library were located around the cloister. [Fig. 30] There was no shared dormitory, but cells in which the brothers also devoted themselves to study. Usually small, these cloisters were sometimes gems of painted decoration; the most famous are the cells at San Marco in Florence painted by Fra Angelico and the Last Supper at the Dominican refectory in Milan by Leonardo da Vinci. Beyond the cloister was

85 Vorreux, 'Les Franciscains'; Chéry, 'Les Dominicains'; Alford and De la Croix, 'L'ordre du Carmel'.

86 Eco, *The Name of the Rose*. Film adaptation: *The Name of the Rose*, by Jean-Jacques Annaud, 1986.

87 Schenkluhn, *Architektur der Bettelorden*; Coomans, 'L'architecture médiévale des ordres mendiants'; Specht and Andraschek-Holzer, *Bettelorden in Mitteleuropa*.

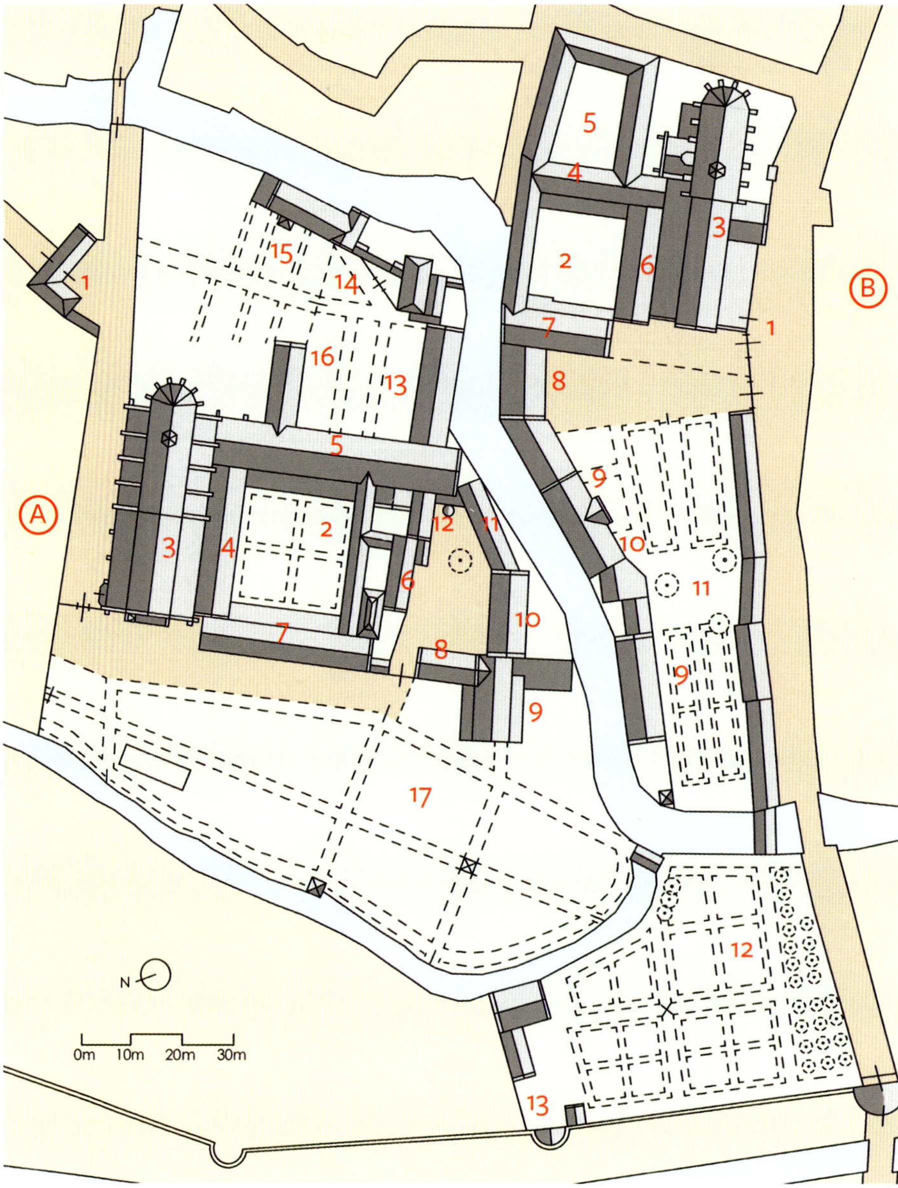

Fig. 30. Dominican and Franciscan friaries located north and south of the river Dyle in the heart of Leuven (Belgium), reconstruction of the seventeenth-century state.
A. Dominicans: 1. gate, 2. cloister, 3. church, 4. dormitory of the philosophy students, 5. sacristy, chapter house and cells of the friars, 6. dormitory of the theology students, 7. school of theology, 8. guesthouse, 9. woodshed, 10. brew house, 11. quarter of the prior, 12. kitchen, 13. library, 14. board of the faculty of theology and chapel, 15. infirmary, 16. small garden, 17. great garden.
B. Franciscans: 1. gate, 2. cloister, 3. church, 4. chapter house and dormitory of the friars, 5. school of theology, 6. library, 7. refectory, 8. kitchen, 9. guesthouse, 10. infirmary, 11. front garden, 12. back garden, 13. first city wall and tower.
[© THOC]

Fig. 31. Franciscan friary of Santa Croce and the Pazzi Chapel in Florence (Italy), by Filippo Brunelleschi, 1442-43.
[© John Kellerman / Alamy Stock Photo]

the street, a stream, sometimes a garden with an infirmary, but, whatever the case, no farm or workshops. Dominican and Franciscan nunneries were different because the female branches of the mendicant orders had no active apostolates in towns but were cloistered contemplative sisters.

The competition between mendicant orders was marked in particular by their efforts to court the favour of patrician families and convince them to have themselves buried in their churches. These burials were the principal source of revenue for mendicant friars who found particularly ingenious ways of increasing the numbers of tombs in their friaries.[88] The great friaries of Santa Croce and Santa Maria Novella in Florence, or San Zanipolo and the Frari in Venice, are majestic examples of this. [Fig. 31] Some friaries began to specialise in the thirteenth century, especially those established in university towns, and developed proper faculties of scholastic theology.[89] In Paris, the friaries of the Dominicans (the *Jacobins*) and the Franciscans (the *Cordeliers*) were

88 Bruzelius, *Preaching, Building, and Burying.*
89 Schenkluhn, *Ordines studentes.*

intellectual centres whose influence extended far beyond their borders, like the work of the Dominican Saint Thomas Aquinas († 1274).

From the end of the fifteenth century, Spanish and Portuguese mendicant orders embarked on the colonial conquest. They became the evangelists of Latin America and Asia and exported their architectural models there. Unlike the friaries of Europe that had to adapt to pre-existing towns, the first friaries of the missions formed part of the very foundations of colonial towns. Their more regular morphology, larger scale and style were part of the ideology of the colonial, conquering, Catholic and centralising power.

Few early mendicant monastic complexes survive because most have been rebuilt or converted over the centuries. Moreover, during the various suppressions of religious orders that have marked history, mendicant convents were often demolished due to their favourable urban location and property speculation [Fig. 86]. The majority of friaries that survived did so because of later reuses. [see Chapters 22 to 26]

10. The Beguinage

In the thirteenth century, an entirely original female movement, that of the Beguines, developed in the urbanised regions of Northern Europe, giving rise to a specific architectural type, the beguinage. The origins of this movement lay in the spontaneous grouping of women who, rejecting the two paths offered by society – marriage or a life devoted to God – imagined a third way, that of 'semi-religiosity'. Small groups of Beguines, living together in houses called 'convents', served a parish, hospital or the needy. They lived off their work, took no vows and retained the option of marrying or embracing a more standard religious life. It goes without saying that this informal movement of women was considered difficult to supervise by the male Church and was not popular, to the extent that Pope Clement V banned the Beguines in 1312. Protected by bishops and local authorities, however, Beguines survived in the former Low Countries and the Prince-Bishopric of Liège,[90] thanks to the development of a new architectural type that allowed them to be controlled.[91]

This saw the building of beguinages, like specific neighbourhoods in their own right, which were usually founded on the outskirts of towns before being swallowed up by the urban extensions of the late Middle Ages. Once refined, the architecture favoured enclosure and mutual social control. The beguinages were surrounded by a wall with a gate, and owned a church and a cemetery, as well as individual houses for affluent Beguines, convents in which poor Be-

90 Roughly the area now represented by Belgium, The Netherlands, Luxembourg and Northern France (Lille, Valenciennes, Arras).

91 Simons, *Cities of Ladies*.

Fig. 32. The Beguinage of Our Lady Ter Hooyen in Ghent (Belgium): the baroque church, four convents and some 100 houses are arranged around a central courtyard and neighbouring streets. [After Clement, Ghobert and Huart, *Les anciennes constructions*, vol. 4, 1919, 135, and <https://kleinbegijnhof-gent.wixsite.com>]

- church and chapels
- superior's house
- presbytery
- beguines' houses
- individual gardens
- common space
- infirmary
- convents
- river

guines lived, and an infirmary. [Fig. 32] The beguinages allowed hundreds of women of humble beginnings to live in a sort of marginality that was both controlled and protected, combining manual labour with personal devotion, thus escaping misery, prostitution and heresies. By its morphology, location and principle of differentiation if not exclusion, the fourteenth-century beguinage had something of a ghetto about it. Beguinages flourished for a second time in the Southern Low Countries during the heyday of the Counter-Reformation

Fig. 33. Two types of 'introverted' houses in the Beguinage of Leuven (Belgium): house with high windows and house with walled front garden, sixteenth and seventeenth centuries.
[© THOC]

in the seventeenth century, leading to the reconstruction of numerous houses and some churches. After a romantic renewal in the nineteenth century, the movement slowly disappeared during the twentieth century. These large beguinages can be found first and foremost in Flanders and Brabant (Belgium); thirteen were listed as World Heritage sites in 1998.[92]

Beguines lived together in houses, went to church every day, and otherwise participated in the economic life of the town or city, notably by producing and bleaching textiles. Two different types of beguinage morphology can be found. On the one hand, the courtyard beguinage, in which the church stands in the middle of a vast open space around which the houses are arranged. On the other, the street beguinage, in which the houses form streets and blocks. Some large beguinages combine a courtyard and streets. [Fig. 32] In all cases, there is no cloister. Beguine houses can be described as 'introverted', in other words, protecting the inhabitants from external eyes by their very form and layout. Either the houses do not overlook the street and are preceded by a walled garden; or, when they do overlook the street, the ground floor windows are sufficiently high up that passers-by cannot look through them. [Fig. 33]

92 Van Aerschot and Heirman, *Flemish Beguinages, World Heritage*. The Dutch beguinages (Amsterdam, Breda etc.) are not included.

Fig. 34. Sint-Annahofje in Leiden (The Netherlands), founded in 1492, seventeenth-century houses. [© THOC]

Semi-religious female movements similar to those of the Beguines developed across Europe but without adopting the architectural style of the beguinage. Numerous communities of lay women were transformed into regular convents, living around a cloister. In Spain, Latin America and the Philippines, the Beaterios, especially for the purpose of welcoming women who had broken their marriage vows and repentant prostitutes, played a social role comparable to that of the beguinage. Beaterios, however, more closely resembled educational institutions, with four wings and a chapel around a courtyard, than a beguinage.[93]

Conversely, from the end of the fifteenth century, foundations for the elderly and the poor adopted a morphology similar to that of the beguinages. The Hofjes in Dutch towns (Leiden, Haarlem, Amsterdam, The Hague, etc.) were private charitable foundations, usually comprising twelve or fifteen small houses around a courtyard with a pump, inside a block and accessible through a door. [Fig. 34] The internal garden courtyards and introverted nature of the Hofjes derive from the monastic cloister. Each foundation was run by 'regents' who would gather in the upper room of the gatehouse. After the French Revolution, the Hofjes were managed by the municipal public

93 Socolow, *The Women of Colonial Latin America*, 90-111; Santiago, *To Love and to Suffer*, 87-172; Muñoz Fernández, *Beatas y santas neocastellanas*.

assistance.[94] In Augsburg (Bavaria), the rich banker Jakob Fugger founded a social housing complex in 1516 that consisted of 67 houses, an infirmary and a chapel to house the city's poor. Like a beguinage, the Fuggerei was laid out along the streets and enclosed by a wall pierced by a gatehouse.[95]

11. The Hôtel-Dieu

Hospitality and charity towards the sick and poor is an essential aspect of Christian works and provides us with a key to a contextual understanding of monasticism. As a result, abbeys had infirmaries for members of the community but also for lay people who came to request hospitality.[96] The welcoming of guests is an essential point in the Rule of Saint Benedict. Military orders initially had a vocation of hospitality aimed at welcoming pilgrims. However, it was in the towns of the twelfth and thirteenth centuries that institutions for the needy, sick, elderly, lepers, plague victims, etc. developed. Their names were defined depending on their specialisation: hospice, Hôtel-Dieu, leprosarium, lazaretto, almshouse, etc. These were not monasteries or convents in the strict sense, but, until the late eighteenth century, these hospital institutions were almost always served by religious communities of hospitaller sisters or brothers who, in the name of the charity of Christ, cared for the sick and helped them to die.[97] [Fig. 35]

Two very different examples are sufficient to illustrate the principle of the architectural type of the Hôtel-Dieu or hospice: the Saint John's Hospital in Bruges and the Hôtel-Dieu in Beaune. The Saint John's Hospital in Bruges is one of the oldest hospital complexes in Europe.[98] Founded in around 1150, it consists of several large naves built as the hospital developed. The beds were lined up in parallel sick wards. [Fig. 36] One of these wards ended in a chapel as the patient had to have the opportunity to see an altar, to attend mass and, if possible, to find meaning for his or her suffering. In addition to the large sick wards and chapel, the hospital included a building for the hospital community, which contained an enclosed garden, a large kitchen, a pharmacy and administrative areas. The Bruges hospital is a remarkable example of growth in an urban setting, without a pre-established plan, through the addition of extra naves according to need and topographical possibilities. It continued to develop until the nineteenth century and is now a museum.

94 Wilms Floet, *Het hofje*.
95 Tietz-Strödel, *Die Fuggerei in Augsburg*.
96 Lindemann-Marz, *Infirmarien - Kranken- und Sterbehäuser der Mönche*.
97 Leistikow, *Ten Centuries of European Hospital Architecture*; Craemer, *Das Hospital als Bautyp des Mittelalters*.
98 Buyle, Dehaeck and Deveseleer, eds, *L'architecture hospitalière en Belgique*, 26-35 and 110-115.

Fig. 35. Gasthuis hospital in Aarschot (Belgium) served by the Grey Sisters of the Third Order of Saint Francis, chapel from 1655-1767.
[© THOC]

A perfectly planned architectural complex around a rectangular courtyard, the Hôtel-Dieu or hospital in Beaune was the exact opposite of the hospital in Bruges. A private foundation of the mid-fifteenth century, it was built in a single phase by the chancellor of the Duke of Burgundy in 1443-52. The large sick ward, with a single nave, ended in a chapel, while three small sick rooms could be found in the other wings. [Fig. 37] The community rooms were located between the sick rooms: kitchen, pharmacy, cellar, the sisters' refectory, the mother superior's office and a well in the centre of the courtyard. Four spiral staircases led to the first floor. Here the architecture contributed brilliantly to the order of the institution.[99] However, neither in Beaune nor Bruges was there a cloister.

Thanks to the evolution of healthcare and prophylaxis from the Enlightenment period onwards, as well as the secularisation of the entire public assistance sector after the French Revolution, the Hôtel-Dieu with convent began to disappear in towns in the early nineteenth century. For example, the large Hôtel-Dieu complex in Paris, located on the Île de la Cité, was converted into a modern hospital during the nineteenth century, although a community of Augustinian sisters remained attached to it until 1908. The many new hospital

99 Viollet-le-Duc, *Dictionnaire raisonné*, vol. 6, 99-120 (article Hôtel-Dieu).

Fig. 36. Saint John's Hospital in Bruges (Belgium), thirteenth-century large sick ward, painting by Johannes Beerblock, eighteenth century.
[Stedelijke Musea Brugge, © Lukas - Art in Flanders / photo Hugo Maertens]

congregations that came into being during the nineteenth century adapted to rational buildings such as those defined by committees of doctors and architects.[100] These favoured hospitals with pavilions linked by galleries because they met with the scientific approach to medicine, care and hygiene. [Fig. 47] From the late nineteenth century onwards, the multi-story hospital block type serviced by elevators began to replace the pavilion hospital.

100 Buyle, Dehaeck and Deveseleer, eds, *L'architecture hospitalière en Belgique.*

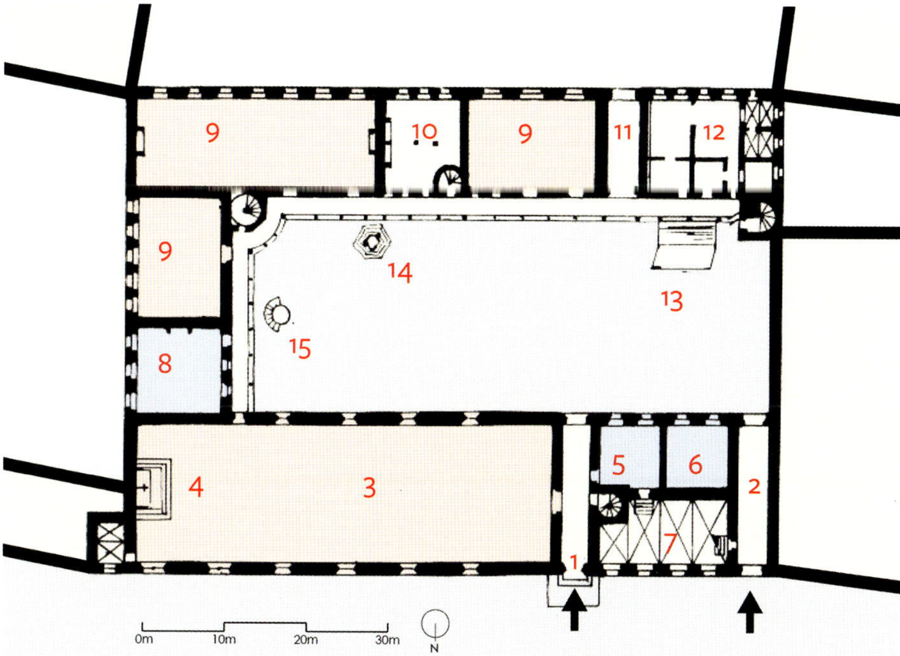

Fig. 37. The Hospices de Beaune (France), built in 1443-52, was served by a community of nuns: 1. main entrance, 2. service passageway, 3. sick ward or room of the poor, 4. altar, 5. nuns' refectory, 6. office of the superior, 7. cellar, 8. novices' room, 9. room of the sick, 10. kitchen, 11. passageway to the garden, 12. pharmacy, 13. wash house, 14. well, 15. chair.
[E.E. Viollet le-Duc, *Dictionnaire raisonné de l'architecture française du XIe au XVIe siècle*, vol. 6, 114]

community sick service garden

12. The College

With the Protestant Reformation – Calvinist, Lutheran and Anglican – and the wars of religion, the sixteenth century was a period of great crisis, rupture and questioning in Europe. The Reformation was followed by the Counter-Reformation, whereby the Catholic Church provided itself with the spiritual and material tools to begin a partial re-conquest of the regions acquired from the various reformed confessions and to initiate a profound religious renaissance. The decisions of the Counter-Reformation were taken during the sessions of the Council of Trent, from 1545 to 1563.

The religious orders of the Middle Ages suffered greatly from the crisis in the Church and the wars of religion in the sixteenth century. On the one hand, religious orders and institutes were simply abolished in countries that became Protestant: England, Scotland, the Northern Low Countries, Scandinavia and Northern Germany. On the other hand, in countries that remained Catholic, well-established orders were reformed from within and new orders were created in response to the new challenges of the Counter-Reformation. The priorities included training secular clergy and young people. This led to the creation of teaching congregations in the sixteenth century: the most famous of these were undoubtedly the Society of Jesus (or Jesuits), founded in 1540 by Saint Ignatius of Loyola († 1556)[101] and the Order of Saint Ursula (or Ursulines), founded in 1535 by Saint Angela Merici († 1540). In the following century, the Brothers of the Christian Schools, founded in 1684 by Saint Jean-Baptiste de La Salle († 1719), were devoted to educating children from poorer backgrounds.[102] These religious institutes were no longer contemplative or predicative monastic orders under the direction of an abbot or prior. Their members were active in the world and had a certain mobility within a network of religious houses with colleges run by superiors or rectors.

The nineteenth century saw a new wave of the founding of religious teaching congregations and institutes for men and women about which there is no room to go into detail here.[103] The majority of these new congregations were founded in response to specific social problems of modern society and were focused on 'target audiences'. Some developed remarkably, acquired an international dimension and took part in missionary evangelisation. Examples include the Society of the Sacred Heart of Jesus, founded in 1800 by Saint Madeleine-Sophie Barat († 1865) for the education of young women, as well as the work of Saint John Bosco († 1888), founder in 1854 of the Society of Saint Francis de Sales (or Salesians) and the Daughters of Mary Auxiliatrix (Salesian Sisters), and the work of Saint Marcellin Champagnat († 1840), founder in 1836 of the Little Brothers of Mary (Marists).

These religious institutes built schools that can be considered a specific architectural type, which we will refer to here as a 'college' in reference to the secondary and university Jesuit teaching establishments. [Fig. 38] Besides colleges, the Jesuits also had 'professed houses', seminaries, novitiates, residences and missions.[104] Under the old regime, Jesuits colleges were necessarily made up of three parts – church, buildings for the community and those for the students – organised around courtyards that were not cloisters.[105] [Fig. 39] The church, which was the most demonstrative and richest building, was not reserved for the fathers and pupils, but also served for preaching to the congregation and confession. The community buildings included a parlour,

101 The Jesuits set out their pedagogical mission in the *Ratio studiorum* (1599). Lacouture, *Les Jésuites*; Egido López, Burrieza Sánchez and Revuelta González, *Los Jesuitas en España*; Rideau, 'Saint Ignace et la Compagnie de Jésus'.

102 Poutet, 'Les Frères des Écoles chrétiennes'.

103 De Maeyer, Leplae and Schmiedl, eds, *Religious Institutes in Western Europe*; and: <http://kadoc.kuleuven.be/relins/be/>.

104 Evans, *Monastic Architecture in France*, 124-139; Bösel and Karner, *Jesuitenarchitektur in Italien*; Álvaro Zamora, Ibáñez Fernández and Criado Mainar, eds, *La arquitectura jesuítica*.

105 Complete preserved case: Genicot and Coomans, 'Les bâtiments des jésuites à Namur'.

Fig. 38. Courtyard of Colegió do Espirito Santo of the Jesuit University of Évora (Portugal), late sixteenth century.
[© THOC]

a refectory, a common room, a library, individual rooms for the fathers, an infirmary and the garden. The college buildings consisted of classrooms and a theatre around another courtyard. At colleges that welcomed in-house students there were also dormitories and bedrooms as well as a refectory.

The architectural principle of these teaching establishments was that of several storey buildings arranged around courtyards. These were not cloisters in the strict sense, but, by retaining the principle of closed and structuring space, were favourable to order and discipline. [Fig. 40] Horizontal circulation was provided by corridors and vertical circulation by stairwells. Internal regulations defined access to the various areas.

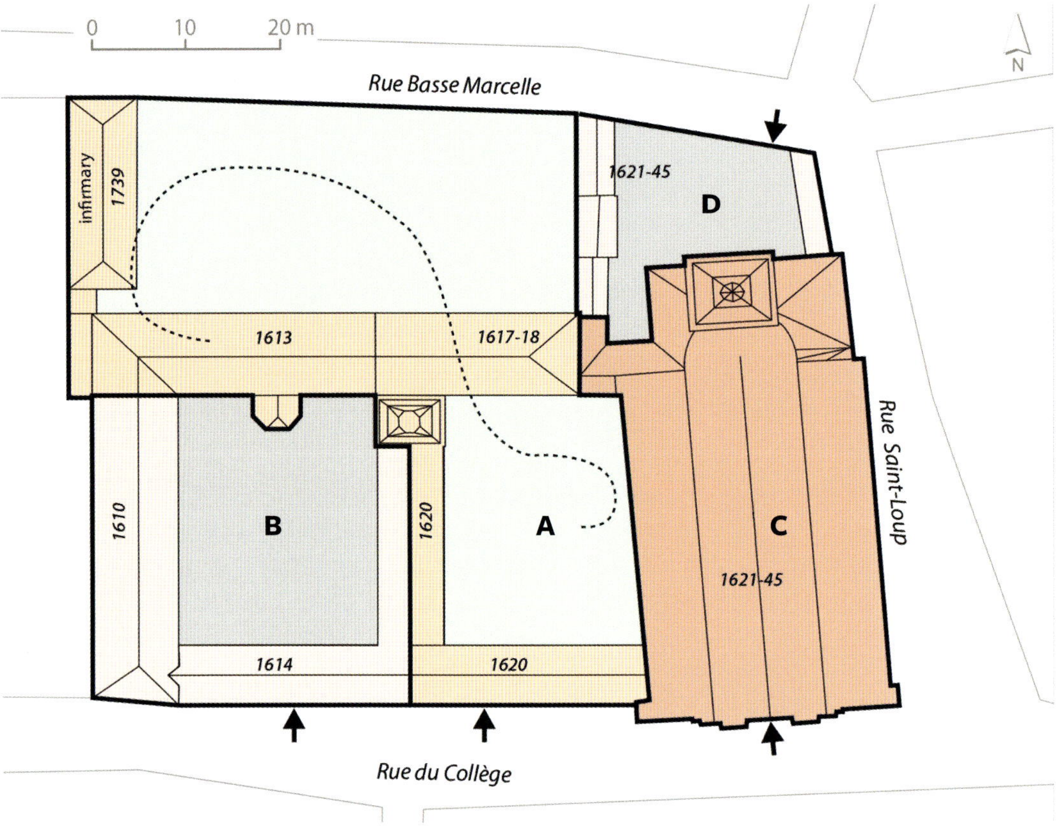

Fig. 39. Jesuit house, church and college in Namur (Belgium) by brother Pieter Huyssens, 1611-45 and 1739. [© THOC]

A. fathers SJ
B. school
C. church
D. service

buildings of the community
courtyard
garden
entrances

The Jesuits built many colleges and some university faculties in Europe. In Spain, the huge college at Monforte de Lemos, built between 1592 and 1624 was reminiscent of the courtyard composition and central church of El Escorial [Fig. 42]. In France, the Collège Royal Henry-le Grand at La Flèche, founded in 1604 with its five courtyards and gardens, was the most prestigious Jesuit teaching institution in the country. [Fig. 41] An important missionary order, the Society of Jesus founded numerous colleges in Asia and the New World, in particular, the *Reductiones* in the province of Paraguay for the Guaraní people.[106] Suppressed in 1763-73, the Society of Jesus lost all its colleges, religious houses and churches. Many colleges were taken over by the local authorities.

106 Film *The Mission*, by Roland Joffé, 1986.

Fig. 40. Courtyard of the Jesuit college of Graz (Austria), seventeenth century, now the diocesan seminary. [© Image Broker / Alamy Stock Photo]

Re-established by the pope in 1814, the Society of Jesus redeveloped significantly in the nineteenth and twentieth centuries and now has some 170 universities and university colleges around the world.

Thanks to their morphology and layout, colleges shared some features with barracks and prisons with courtyards. It is significant that many monasteries were converted into schools, prisons and military establishments in the early nineteenth century [see Chapters 25 and 26]. The college type had already been developed under the influence of the Enlightenment but the new educational and public health theories of the nineteenth century fixed the architectural principle of wings with several floors and open courtyards, efficient circulation and light. The school model of closed courtyards, distant descendants of the monastery, disappeared in the twentieth century.

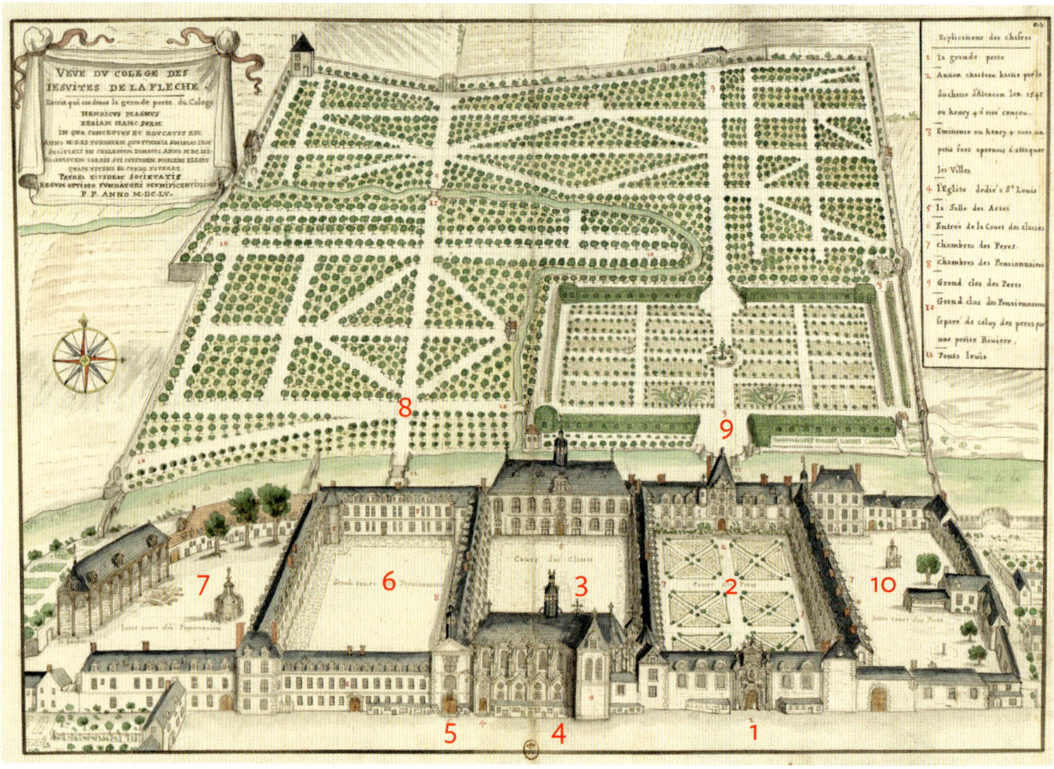

Fig. 41. Royal Jesuit College in La Flèche (France), founded by King Henry IV, built by architect Louis Métézeau and brother Étienne Martellange, 1607-60s. Buildings and courtyards: 1. main entrance, 2. courtyard of the Jesuit fathers, 3. courtyard of the college, 4. Saint Louis church, 5. entrance to the college, 6. courtyard of the in-house students, 7. service courtyard of the in-house students, 8. garden of the students, 9. garden of the Jesuit fathers, 10. service courtyard of the Jesuit fathers.

13. The Palace

To a greater or lesser extent, medieval abbeys always maintained links with political powers, although these varied in their intensity. The level could range from the local lord who had helped to found the abbey and whose family were buried in the church, to royal and imperial abbeys, whose superiors were part of the sovereign's entourage. The phenomenon of the burial of lay people in monasteries, as well as funerary abbeys and necropolises, will be discussed later [see Chapter 18]. Royal and imperial abbeys were visited by sovereigns because it was part of their policy of representation, while the abbeys concerned made efforts to maintain this privileged link that guaranteed them prestige and favours.

From an architectural point of view, royal and imperial abbeys not only had to have infrastructures capable of accommodating the sovereign and his court for several days but their architecture also expressed their role and political status. At Carolingian and Ottonian imperial abbeys, such as those at Corvey, Nivelles and Saint Riquier [Fig. 14], the presence of a westwork with a tribune and imperial hall accessible from staircase turrets made the abbey's status as a 'landmark' clear. In the regions of conquest, whether in Spain and Portugal during the *reconquista* or in Central Europe, sovereigns used abbeys as pawns on a chessboard on the scale of vast territories. In the feudal world, founded on the ownership of land and bonds of allegiance, sovereigns trusted in their abbeys more than in their barons. During the conquests, abbeys were founded and generously endowed with land; sovereigns would visit them and fund constructions that expressed their status. These abbeys found themselves in difficulty if they lost this role, either because the region in which they were located had lost its strategic interest or because a new dynasty had taken power and instituted a new policy by using other abbeys.

In the mid-sixteenth century, King Philip II of Spain († 1598) built the abbey-palace of El Escorial in the mountains near Madrid in keeping with a new architectural concept that would have considerable influence on monastic architecture.[107] [Fig. 42] The Catholic kingdom of Spain after the *reconquista* had unheard-of wealth since the discovery of the New World, which allowed King Philip II to build a dynastic abbey that expressed his identity. The project was in keeping with the ambition and means of the king, who had it built rapidly: the first stone was laid in 1563 and construction was completed in 1584. The abbey was populated by Hieronymite monks, an order of hermits comparable to the Carthusians that only existed in Spain and was linked to the crown. In addition, El Escorial is home to the largest collection of relics of saints in the world (570 reliquaries spread throughout the monastery).

Designed by the architects Juan Bautista de Toledo and Juan de Herrera, El Escorial was the first monastic complex built on axial symmetry. It was not a cloister but the dynastic funerary church, its large dome and royal crypt that formed its centre: the axis of composition crosses the middle of the main façade, the courtyard of the church, the church and the king's apartments behind the choir. Because prayer, piety and memory were a prerequisite to power, the bedroom of the 'Catholic king', which was reminiscent of a monastic cell, had a direct view towards the tabernacle of the high altar.[108]

The rest of the complex consists of orthogonal buildings around courtyards, forming a grid-like plan inside a large rectangle punctuated by corner

107 Kubler, *Building the Escorial*; von der Osten-Sacken, *San Lorenzo el Real de el Escorial*; Braunfels, *Monasteries of Western Europe*, 175-200.

108 Unlike at Versailles, where it was the bedroom of the King of France that was the centre of the main axis; the chapel there is lateral and did not have a funerary function but primarily played a theatrical role in court ritual.

Fig. 42. Royal Monastery of San Lorenzo de El Escorial (Spain), by architects Juan Bautista de Toledo and Juan de Herrera, 1563-84.
[© Marie Hautcoeur]

towers. There is no enclosing wall, but its monumental scale, grandiose landscape and quasi-military style gives the complex the appearance of a citadel and palace. The apartments of the queen and other relatives were distributed around the north cloister. Two hundred monks occupied the south section, around the large cloister, each with their own apartment; they were like soldiers in the service of the king and Christ. In the front section there was a college for the training of the elite in the service of the king and the Church, while the south section was home to the abbey's most prestigious rooms: the refectory and, most importantly, the library. These various areas were linked by corridors, galleries and stairwells, access to which was regulated and in which processions took place. El Escorial was a place of absolute order: everyone had his or her place according to a well-oiled court ritual, that of an absolute Catholic dynasty whose power was based on the synthesis of royalty, monasticism, the idea of nationhood and dynastic memory. El Escorial became an archetype that inspired other monarchs, notably the kings of Portugal, who built the Palácio Nacional de Mafra in 1717-30 and filled it with Franciscans.

The phenomenon of large Baroque abbeys linked to absolute royal and Catholic power led to some sixty extraordinary abbeys in Austria, Switzerland and in Southern Germany (Bavaria, Swabia, Franconia and Rhineland).[109] The idea of a revival of order and monarchy in a society profoundly ravaged by the Thirty Years' War (1618-48) and by the Ottoman thrust across the Danube plain as far as the gates of Vienna (1683) lent weight to these abbeys. Veritable 'cities of God' built on dominant points in the landscape, these abbeys imposed themselves physically and economically over vast areas. The order of the architecture expressed the spiritual and temporal order: the abbeys were examples of good management and worked for the common good, in other words, the restoration of Christian society. There were enough monks to fill these great abbeys that the sovereigns loved to visit.

The Benedictine abbey of Einsiedeln (Switzerland), designed by the architect Caspar Moosbrugger in 1704 and completed in 1770, can be considered the prototype of the great Baroque abbeys. The Benedictine abbey of Weingarten (Baden-Württemberg), designed by Moosbrugger and Franz Beer around 1750, reached perfection in the idea of order and symmetry of the monastic city centred on its church. The most spectacular of all is undoubtedly the Benedictine abbey of Melk (Austria), built in the Middle Ages on a hill in a loop of the Danube Valley and a symbol of resistance to the Ottomans. It was completely rebuilt from 1702 on the orders of the Emperor of Austria by the architect Jacob Prandtauer. [Fig. 43] Its form was defined by its site: a first courtyard with a military appearance is flanked by two artillery bastions; below, the domestic courtyard is dominated by the abbey-palace forming the courtyard of honour; the church was built along the axis of the promontory, flanked by the cloister and the monastic buildings; the apartments of the emperor are on the other side of the church. The highlight of the composition is the majestic staging of the end of the promontory: an open courtyard on the façade of the church, framed by the imperial hall (Kaisersaal) and the library, the two most prestigious buildings. Finally, at the end of the courtyard, a triumphal arch opens onto the Danube Valley.

Such projects depended on the will of a sovereign and would not necessarily be continued by their successor. The greatest projects therefore remained unfinished. Construction of the Augustinian abbey of Klosterneuburg, for example, undertaken in 1730 by Emperor Charles VI, who wanted to found an Austrian El Escorial, came to a halt on his death in 1740. The library became an increasingly important component in the large male abbeys of the eighteenth century.[110] They were not only places of prestige, but also places of

109 Schütz, *Die kirchliche Barockarchitektur in Bayern und Oberschwaben*; Bauer and Bauer, *Klöster in Bayern*; Braunfels, *Monasteries of Western Europe*, 201-220; Bazin, *Les Palais de la Foi*.

110 Lehman, *Die Bibliotheksräume der deutschen Klöster*.

Fig. 43. Benedictine abbey of Melk overlooking the Danube river (Austria), rebuilt by architect Jakob Prandtauer in 1702-36.
[© aerial-photos.com / Alamy Stock Photo]

science, as the abbeys were not immune to the scientific spirit of the Enlightenment and their communities often included scholars. [Figs 76 and 104]

There was nothing comparable in other countries, certainly not in France, where, from the sixteenth century onwards, most abbots were appointed by the king. These abbots, known as 'commendatory abbots' did not have to be monks; they could hold simultaneously several posts as abbots and, consequently, the income of several abbeys. Some built abbey palaces, sorts of small pleasure castles next to the abbeys, quite unlike the German Baroque abbeys. Another consequence was the will to reform certain abbeys that rejected the 'commend' and founded, in particular, the Benedictine congregation of Saint Maur (Mauristes) in 1618 and the Cistercian Order of Strict Observance (Trappists) of Abbot Armand de Rancé († 1700).

From the mid-eighteenth century, the spirit of the Enlightenment replaced that of the Counter-Reformation, as the neo-classical style did the Baroque. One might say that reason gradually triumphed over the idea of the City of God and that 'secular prestige' overturned monastic austerity. The large abbeys that had the means demolished their medieval buildings, with the excep-

Fig. 44. Medieval Benedictine abbey of Cluny (France), partially rebuilt in a classical style in the late eighteenth century and partially ruined after 1796.
[© aerial-photos.com / Alamy Stock Photo]

tion of the church, in favour of monastic buildings with a classical style and the appearance of palaces with several storeys, columns and classical pediments. The compositions were regular, symmetrical, ordered and opened onto formal gardens. The expanded and rigorously square cloisters now took their inspiration from royal palaces. The corridors were wide, the stairwells worthy of palaces and the decor sumptuous. The abbeys of Cluny, Cîteaux, Prémontré, Clairvaux, Morimond, Saint Riquier, Saint Denis, Saint Germain in Auxerre and plenty of others were completely transformed, retaining nothing of the prestigious medieval past but their churches.[111] [Fig. 44] Conversely, many abbeys whose incomes were drained by their commendatory abbots were on the brink of material and spiritual bankruptcy.

Belgium, part of the Austrian Southern Low Countries in the eighteenth century, experienced a major wave of abbey reconstruction from the 1760s to 80s that was interrupted by the French Revolution. Wanting to reinject the dormant capital of the abbeys into the economy proper, the emperor and

111 Baud, *Cluny*, 38-49; Plouvier and Saint-Denis, eds, *Pour une histoire monumentale de l'abbaye de Cîteaux*; Bugner, *Cadre architectural et vie monastique des Bénédictins*.

Fig. 45. Benedictine abbey of Gembloux (Belgium), entirely rebuilt by architect Laurent-Benoît Dewez in 1762-79.
[Photo Guy Focant © SPW-Patrimoine]

governors imposed extremely expensive works on the abbeys. This benefited the construction sector and forced the abbeys to sell off part of their land. Laurent-Benoît Dewez, the court architect, orchestrated these works and imposed a rational architecture of neo-classical style that was in keeping with the imperial propaganda influenced by the spirit of the Enlightenment.[112] In the majority of cases, the scenario was that of a clean slate, including the church, and the construction of large symmetrical compositions. At the Trappist abbey of Orval and the Premonstratensian abbey of Heylissem the church was still at the centre of the composition but their façades were those of classical palaces. At the Benedictine abbey of Gembloux, the structuring of the space expressed a sort of disintegration of its components, each of which formed a separate entity dominated by its centrepiece: the monastic buildings with the church, the abbot's quarter with the palace and the farm with the grange. [Fig. 45] There was no longer any order around the cloister but several orders juxtaposed like units with their own logic.

112 Van de Vijver, 'L'architecture dans les Pays-Bas autrichiens et la Principauté de Liège', 131-138.

Fig. 46. Jesuit Saint Michael College in Brussels (Belgium), by architects Alphonse Gellé and Joseph Premont, 1902-12. The residence and courtyard of the Jesuit fathers are left of the church; the college is to the right.
[KADOC, Leuven].

The symmetrical and rational composition of pre-revolutionary neoclassicism became the preferred type throughout the nineteenth and part of the twentieth century. Examples are legion, even on other continents.[113] The church or the chapel was in the middle of the composition while buildings of several storeys developed on both sides forming open courtyards. The cloister galleries were now replaced by corridors.

Distant descendants of El Escorial and the Baroque German abbeys, many religious houses built in the nineteenth century adopted the palace type revised by the rational architectural design theory taught by Jean-Nicolas-Louis Durand.[114] The rational modernity of functional architectural programmes imposed itself on numerous convents and abbeys, as well as on the schools, barracks, hospitals and prisons of the industrial age. In the middle of symmetrical compositions, the church gave complexes a monumentality, a visibility and a feeling of stability in a society secularised after the revolution. [Figs 46 and 47]

113 Noppen and Morisset, 'La renaissance des couvents au Québec'.
114 Durand, *Précis des leçons d'architecture.*

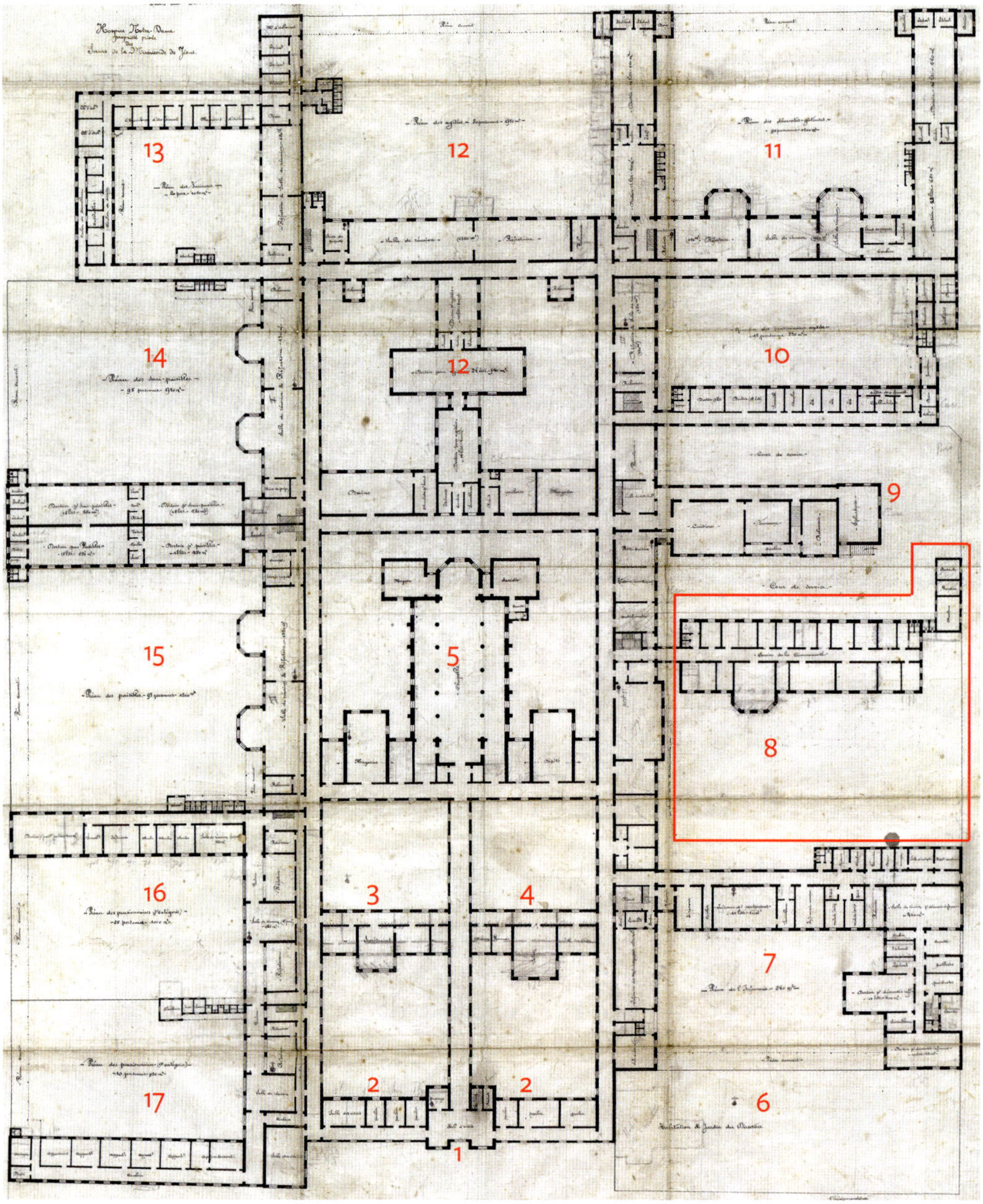

Fig. 47. Rational plan of a hospice for 450 mentally ill women in Sint-Michiels near Bruges (Belgium), served by the Augustinian Sisters of Mercy of Jesus, designed by engineer-architect Jules Coomans, 1906. 1. main entrance, 2. parlours and rooms for visits, 3. secretary and administration, 4. doctors, 5. chapel, 6. location of the director's house, 7. infirmary, 8. convent of the sisters, 9. kitchen and services, 10. section for 15 agitated residents, 11. section for 90 senile demented patients, 12. section for 80 agitated patients, 13. section for 20 furious patients, 14. section for 95 semi-peaceful patients, 15. section for 95 peaceful patients, 16. section for 25 second category residents, 17. section for 10 first category residents. [© Psychiatrisch Instituut Brugge]

14. The House

Diametrically opposed to that of the palace, but also to that of the abbey, the architectural type of the 'house monastery' came into being in the reforming context of the Second Vatican Council (1962-65), with a view to a return to basic communities on the model of the early Christians. In a complete break with the past, it was a plea for the 'religious incognito' of the brotherhood, which played a full part in the world without giving any external sign of its presence. Promoted by the Benedictine Frédéric Debuyst (†2017) in the journal *Art d'Église*, the concept of the 'house monastery', as a 'house for the community' or 'church house' (*domus ecclesiae*), marked the generation of the 1960s and early 1970s.[115] Architecture played an essential role in this, rejecting both the monumentality of the triumphant Church and functionalist modernity. It adopted the silhouette, scale and materials of domestic architecture and aimed to blend into the built environment of urban neighbourhoods or integrate into natural sites.

The monastic world was turned profoundly on its head during the 1960s. A new generation saw the Council as an opening, a liberation even, before experiencing the disappointment inherent in excessive enthusiasm. The abolition of hierarchies within communities in favour of brotherhood, liturgical changes, clothing changes and the adaptation of daily life accompanied architectural transformations that could sometimes be radical. Brother Denis Aubert, the architect of the ecumenical monastic community of Taizé in France, explained:

> A community is a developing living organism, full of surprises; if it allows itself to become imprisoned within a carapace, it risks dying. Instead, it should secrete its skin, which from time to time it takes the risk of moulting. A permanent building site? Almost, one of noise, dust and a certain insecurity, that of a life that is not fixed.[116]

The Benedictine monastery of Saint-André de Clerlande in Ottignies (Belgium) was the first house monastery. [Fig. 48] Built in a wood in 1969-71, it consists of two houses comprising cells, guest rooms, workplaces and a chapel for the domestic Eucharist. There is no cloister. Its utopian ambition was to become the nucleus of a small monastic village, with houses for sisters and multi-family homes all in harmony with nature, described as an 'ecological experience'.[117] To the two houses only a chapel was added, built in 1982 in the same spirit of meditative and discreet integration with the site. The concept of the house

115 Debuyst, 'Contrastes monastiques'; Bekaert, *In een of ander huis* [In one house or another].
116 Aubert, 'Habiter des maisons', 219.
117 Debuyst, 'A Short Dialectic of the "House Monastery"'; Cosse, 'The Monastery of Saint Andrew at Ottignies'; Debuyst, 'The New Chapel at the Monastery of Clerlande'.

Fig. 48. Benedictine house monastery of Saint-André de Clerlande in Ottignies (Belgium), by architect Jean Cosse, 1969-82.
[© THOC]

monastery of Clerlande and its project for monastic life differed completely from that of La Tourette by Le Corbusier, still influenced by the prosperity of 1950s monasticism.[118] [Fig. 83]

The Benedictines of Saint-Wandrille de Fontenelle in Normandy, unable to restore the ruins of their Gothic abbey church, acquired a large late medieval barn in another location. They dismantled it and rebuilt it near the cloister of their abbey. This conversion of vernacular architecture into a church took place in 1968, the year of the cultural revolution that shook Western society.

In 1975-76, the Dominican friary of Froidmont in Rixensart moved into an old, eighteenth-century courtyard farm and, with the support of the local parish, developed a collective housing project. Despite the formal resemblance between the rectangular courtyard farm and a cloister, the project rejected any form of enclosure and opened the courtyard up to everyone. [Fig. 49] The various functions of the friary – hospitality, lodgings and a monastic and public library – occupied three sides, while the large barn became the parish church. On this occasion, monastic modernity was intended to be participatory, authentic and a part of the life of modern society.[119] This experience of a parish house monastery in a former farm was unique. Typical of the spirit of 1968, it did not survive its generation and the frairs left in 2009.

118 Debuyst, 'Monasteries. Places for a New Christian 'Art of Living'?'; Debuyst, 'Contrastes'.
119 Kroll, 'The Dominican Monastery at Froidmont (Rixensart)'; Debuyst, 'L'église Saint-Étienne à Froidmont'.

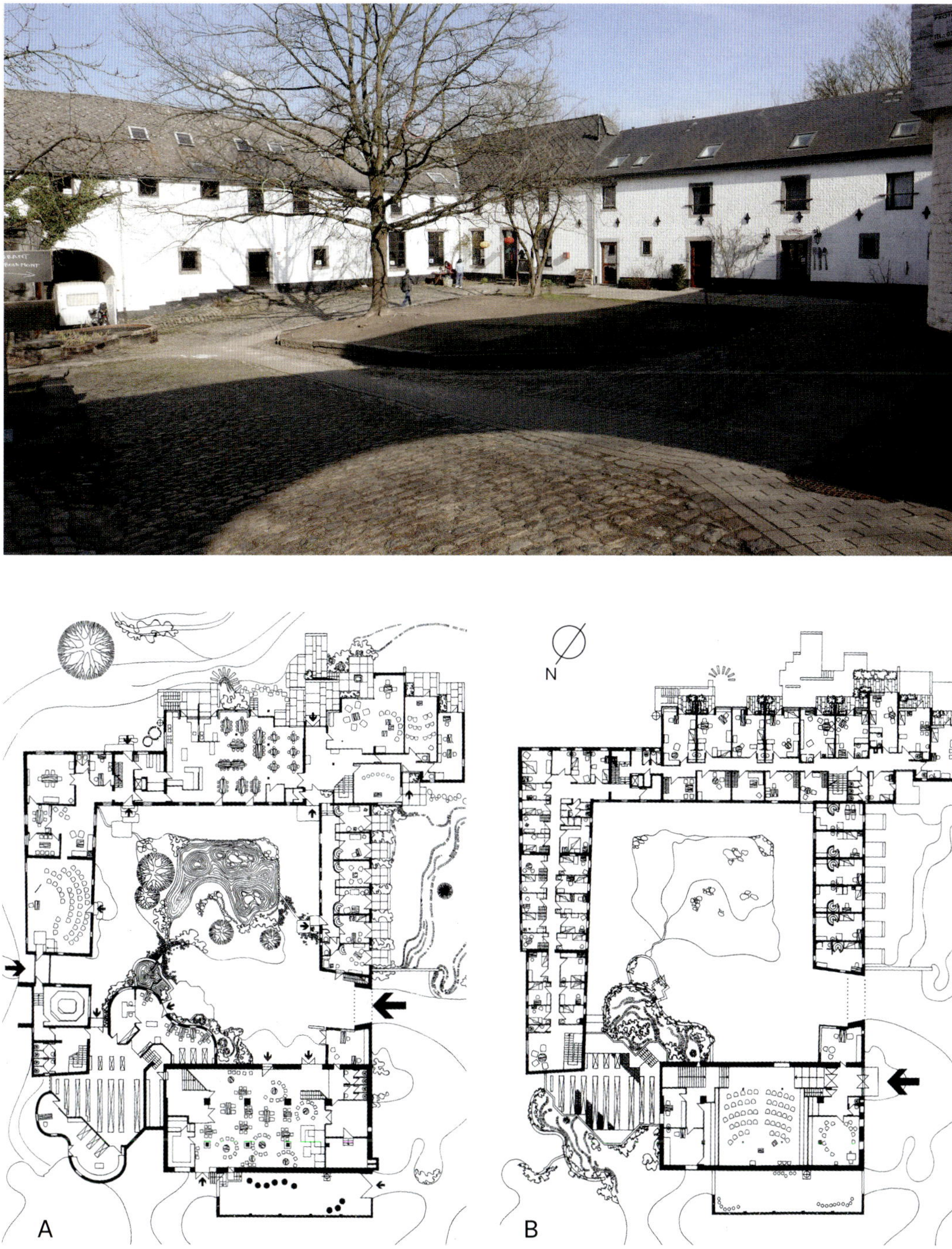

Fig. 49. Dominican friary of Froidmont in Rixensart (Belgium) by architect Lucien Kroll, 1975-76.
A. Lower storey; B. Upper storey.
[Kroll, 'The Dominican Monastery at Froidmont', 1976. Photo ©THOC]

Fig. 50. Cistercian abbey of Sénanque (France), founded in 1148 in a remote valley in Provence.
[© Age Fotostock / Alamy Stock Photo]

CHARACTERS

EMBODYING THE SACRED

Beyond the architectural components the origins of which have been examined in the first section and the architectural types described in the second section, what is it that distinguishes monastic architecture? This third section examines the characters that touch upon the profound essence of monastic architecture, its 'way of being'. These are not simply characteristics as they affect all monasteries in one way or another, regardless of their type. Consequently, we will talk about 'characters' rather than 'characteristics'.

Characters play a full part in the tradition of monasteries and religious institutes and therefore exert an essential influence on the architecture. They allow us to understand the evolution of monastic architecture over space and time, taking into account the various identities of the establishments. Moreover, monasteries also have a sacred dimension [see Introduction].[120] Six characters are addressed in this third section: place and stability, enclosure and gender, liturgy and identity, death and memory, scale and growth, and finally, style.

15. Place and Stability

Place is obviously the first constituent character of the identity of a religious establishment. The choice of the place of foundation of an abbey – depending on practical, political and spiritual criteria – is a founding act that, in a way, expresses the very paradox of monastic life. It is the most radical

120 Veilleux, 'What makes a Monastery a Sacred Place?'.

version of the utopia of the Kingdom of God, or the Heavenly Jerusalem, to which every Christian is invited by converting but, at the same time, must also be a physical space with material constraints.[121] Monasticism implies a social withdrawal from the world, perfectly symbolised by the desert, which was both a paradise where monks lived in harmony with the cosmos and a place of struggle against temptation and the deep self. [Fig. 4] This withdrawal from the world makes the monastery a place of death and resurrection in which the monk enters a new life in Christ, that anticipates the Kingdom of God [see also Chapter 16]. At the same time, each settlement belonged, from its foundation, to a precise geographical, historical and social context. Each monastery developed its own specific material culture by interacting with its rural or urban surroundings.[122]

Built in the image of the Heavenly Jerusalem, the cloister and abbey were, in the eyes of the monk, built for eternity. When he entered the abbey the monk knew that, barring any unforeseen circumstances, he would spend his entire life there and be buried within its enclosure. This attachment to the place of 'monastic stability' was therefore essential as it had a profound community dimension.

> Stability, according to Benedictine spirituality, is the visible, physical expression of a deeper reality – that of communion. It is around that reality of communion that the whole way of life of the monastic community is built and it is around it that the architecture of the monastery develops. It is impossible to understand traditional monastic architecture without taking this into consideration. First of all, it is the aspiration to a communion with God in contemplative prayer. That communion is then expressed and lived out in a communion with brethren within a local community. That community opens itself to the local Church and the Church at large, and also to the world, especially to the people around the monastery and to guests. Finally, it includes a communion with nature, with the environment and with the whole cosmos. The architecture of a monastery is meant to foster all those levels of communion.[123]

The founding act of the choice of a place for the establishment of a monastery truly sanctifies that place. It has a symbolic spatiotemporal dimension of real and imaginary space that is immutable and eternal. Furthermore, once chosen, the place is sanctified by a variety of rituals that punctuate the phases of consecration, of which the dedication of the church is the most important.

121 Sheldrake, *Spaces for the Sacred*, 90-118 (monasteries as utopias).
122 Gilchrist, *Contemplation and Action: the Other Monasticism.*
123 Veilleux, 'What Makes a Monastery a Sacred Place?', 31.

Fig. 51. Monte Cassino Abbey (Italy), origin of the Benedictine order, founded by Saint Benedict of Nursia circa 529 on the top of a hill.
[© Enzo Minchella / Alamy Stock Photo]

Without falling into the romantic theory of the '*genius loci*', it must be admitted that certain places 'between heaven and earth' were predestined thanks to the way in which they elevate the soul and bring man closer to heaven. [Fig. 51] The abbeys of Monte Cassino and Subiaco (Lazio), Mont-Saint-Michel (Normandy), Sacra di San Michele (Piedmont), Mount Carmel (Israel), Santa Maria de Montserrat (Catalonia), Sainte-Marie-Madeleine in Vézelay (Burgundy), Rock of Cashel (Ireland) and many others are built on sacred mountains. These are the 'high places' of monasticism, both literally and figuratively. Since prehistory or Antiquity, many of these mountains had been occupied by the sanctuary of another religion, as well as taking on a spiritual and political dimension within a particular area. The eighteenth-century Baroque abbeys of Bavaria and Austria had a clear political and territorial significance [see Chapter 13]. These extremely spectacular holy places, often packed with pilgrims, continue to exert a strong attraction in the modern world.

Despite its desire for symbolic and physical withdrawal from the world, an abbey was never removed from the world; it was part of a rural or urban landscape and maintained a complex political, economic, social and ecological

Fig. 52. Benedictine abbey of Saint-Martin-du-Canigou (France), founded in 1005 in the Pyrenees. [© Hemis/Alamy Stock Photo]

relationship with its environment.[124] [Fig. 53] An abbey needed an income and its rural economy involved the existence of organised grounds, sometimes several tens of thousands of hectares, as well as an economy suited to the features of the site.[125]

The search for remote and solitary places, like the desert or the Thebaid, lay at the root of the foundation of many abbeys in mountains or on summits, as, for example, the twenty abbeys of Mount Athos in Greece built more than a thousand years ago. Topography was sometimes such a constraint that architects had to be highly ingenious in order to remain faithful to the layout. At Mont-Saint-Michel, monastic functions were layered in the '*Merveille*', a building constructed on three levels on the side of the rock. At Saint-Martin-du-Canigou, the church and cloister extend over two levels. [Fig. 52]

Deep and remote valleys were another form of monastic desert, sought out in particular by the Cistercians, in whose spiritual literature metaphors abound e.g. the valley of tears (in the *Salve Regina* prayer) or the valley as a receptacle for the rain of divine grace.[126] [Fig. 50] More prosaically, a valley is

124 Aston, *Monasteries in the Landscape*.
125 Pressouyre, *L'espace cistercien*.
126 Auberger, *L'unanimité cistercienne primitive*, 87-133.

Fig. 53. Benedictine abbey of Whitby (England) founded in 657 on a cliff overlooking the North Sea. [© Edwin Remsberg / Alamy Stock Photo]

always associated with the presence of water, a factor indispensable to the life of an abbey, as well as something explicitly mentioned in the Rule of Saint Benedict [see Chapter 2]. The material and spiritual were inseparable. The Cistercians had a remarkable mastery of hydraulic techniques and developed sometimes highly complex networks for conveying drinking water and sewage disposal. [Fig. 20] The water was collected, channelled and disposed of; it served the cloister fountain, pools and fish ponds, drove the mills' wheels and carried away waste from the kitchen and the latrines.[127]

The names of many abbeys contain an allusion to the topography of the place or to water. This can be found in all forms and in all languages. These refer primarily to mountains (Mont-Saint-Michel, Mount Grace, Monte Cassino, Montserrat, Hautmont, Mont César, Altenberg, Monte Maria), valleys (Clairvaux, Orval, Chiaravalle, Gnadental, Val-de-Grâce, La Valsainte, Val-Dieu, Val-Saint-Lambert), rivers (La Charité-sur-Loire, Heisterbach, Eberbach), lakes (Saint-Benoît-du-Lac, Noirlac), springs (Bronnbach, Maulbronn), river banks (Hauterive) and fountains (Fontenay, Trois-Fontaines, Fountains, Fontenelle, Fontfroide, Fontevraud, Trefontane, Sept-Fons), to name but a few.

127 Pressouyre and Benoit, *L'hydraulique monastique*.

Fig. 54. Benedictine abbey of Saint Philibert in Tournus (France), established in 875 along the Saône River. [© Hemis/Alamy Stock Photo]

An often crucial aspect of the monastic place is its relationship with the town, in other words with the world. There are many instances that respond to varied and not always serene types of relationships: domination, submission, conflict, and so on. These powerful relationships with political and economic elements evolved with time and urbanisation.

One initial example is that of the towns that built up around abbeys. These spontaneous agglomerations attracted people looking for work in exchange for protection. Taking advantage of the success of pilgrimages, some became market towns, such as Vézelay and Tournus, or sizeable towns such as Sint-Truiden. [Fig. 54] The second scenario is of course that of deliberate foundation in a town, something sought after by mendicant and hospitaller orders from the thirteenth century and by an increasing number of religious institutes over subsequent centuries. The town or city was the site of their apostolate and social action, where they also benefited from military and legal protection. [Fig. 55] A third instance was that of abbeys, friaries and beguinages founded outside towns, such as Saint-Germain-des-Prés and Saint-Martin-des-Champs in Paris, but which were eventually swallowed up and integrated into the growing urban fabric. Monasteries suffered the disadvantages of urban life but also benefited from increased real estate value. The construction of large urban fortifications following developments in artillery prevented the growth of the majority of towns between the sixteenth and nineteenth centuries. A fourth scenario occurred when religious communities, feeling unsafe in their countryside monastery, moved into towns. The former, now abandoned,

Fig. 55. Church and friary of the Jacobins, established by the Dominicans in 1230 in the heart of Toulouse (France).
[© THOC]

monastery would then become a farm whose income contributed to meeting the needs of the new urban monastery.

On the eve of the French Revolution, monasteries, convents, beguinages and other religious establishments owned a significant amount of land in towns, sometimes as much as a quarter of the urban area. The suppression of many religious houses in the late eighteenth century allowed the redistribution of these lands and, in one way or another, was a boon for urban development. The afterlife of these suppressed religious houses is discussed elsewhere [see Chapters 21 to 26].

The question of monastic sites and religious institutes changed over the course of the nineteenth and twentieth centuries. The large estates, mortmain rights and other advantages of the old regime belonged to the past. Some communities managed to recover their sometimes ruined historical sites and spoke of 're-foundation' or even 'resurrection'. The older the monastic community, the more important the relationship to its historical site. The abbeys of Orval and Landévennec, suppressed in the late eighteenth century, were re-founded next to the ruins of their former abbeys in 1926 and 1958 respectively.[128] [Fig. 73] In the majority of cases this was no longer possible because other owners now occupied the sites, the community had not survived or no longer had the means, having lost its estate and income. The phenomenon of the 'reconquest' of secularised sites and abbeys could also be seen in Central Europe and Russia after 1989.[129]

In the nineteenth and twentieth centuries, the question of the sites of many new religious foundations arose in a different way, particularly in an urban setting. The rapid transformations of the industrial and modern city combined with the growth of new active religious institutes and their works (hospitals, schools, etc.) often involved relocation and property speculation. When a religious institute was in a densely built neighbourhood and could no longer extend, it sold its property and moved to the outskirts. Once there, it acquired vast swathes of land, the property value of which would grow with the urban development of the new neighbourhood. The large periurban architectural complexes of the second half of the nineteenth century and interwar years, built according to rational plans on advantageous sites, no longer had the spiritual or mystical significance of the sites of the Middle Ages but expressed the present of the Church in secular society, as well as its success. [Figs 46 and 47] However, for contemplative communities transfer to another site remained an extremely difficult decision to make because the site was part of the identity and history of the abbey, not to mention the cemetery, which also needed to be moved.[130]

128 Soetens, *Orval 1926-1948*; Tranvouez, 'Friches monastiques'.

129 Bellat, 'Les monastères de Russie'.

130 Kinder, 'What makes a Site Sacred?', 196-200 (about the transfer of the monks' cemetery from the abbey of Our Lady of the Valley, RI, to St Joseph's Abbey, Spencer, MA).

16. Enclosure and Gender

The enclosure is a constituent character of a monastery: it is explicitly required by the Rule and is therefore present in all religious houses, including house monasteries [see Chapters 6 to 14]. The cloister, *claustrum*, is the most tangible evidence of this. The desert was the first form of enclosure in this desire for separation from the world (*fuga mundi*). But the enclosure was not just a fence or a physical barrier; it was also social, psychological and spiritual. The enclosure can also be considered a form of 'sexuality contract' guaranteeing the vow of chastity.

> The enclosure exists in all monasteries but its meaning differs greatly depending on whether it is inhabited by men or women. Among men, it refers to all the material means by which the community wishes to protect its solitude and fraternal life from any untimely intervention from the outside world. Among women, the enclosure is enriched with particular significance and takes on a fourfold theological dimension: solitude with Christ, a demand for love in the mystical marriage, a voluntary ascetic dimension and an openness to the world through the prayer of intercession.[131]

It was as a result of this that Saint Thérèse of Lisieux († 1897), a contemplative and cloistered Carmelite, was proclaimed patron saint of the missions in 1927.[132]

A foundation of the order around the cloister, the enclosure had to be both material and effective. The buildings were surrounded by walls, sometimes crenellated and with towers, which prevented both outsiders from entering and members of the community from leaving. The gatehouse, a genuine 'check point', regulated exchanges with the exterior; as a result, there was always an inside and an outside. [Fig. 24] Inside the enclosure, walls provided other subdivisions, in particular between monks and lay brothers, and indicated circulation routes. [Figs 56 and 57] The Rule of Saint Benedict recommended choosing a good monk as a gate keeper.

In contemplative female communities the enclosure has always been at its strictest. High walls, ditches, gates, locked doors, windows placed high enough so that they could not be seen through, and inward-looking beguinage houses were all architectural ways of protecting the monastery from evil, ensuring the inviolability of the place and guaranteeing the virginity of its

131 Brugués, 'La clôture: son sens et son projet dans une vie religieuse'.

132 The film *Thérèse*, by Alain Cavalier, 1986 (based on Thérèse of Lisieux, *The Story of a Soul*, 1898), offers an insight into life in a Carmelite convent.

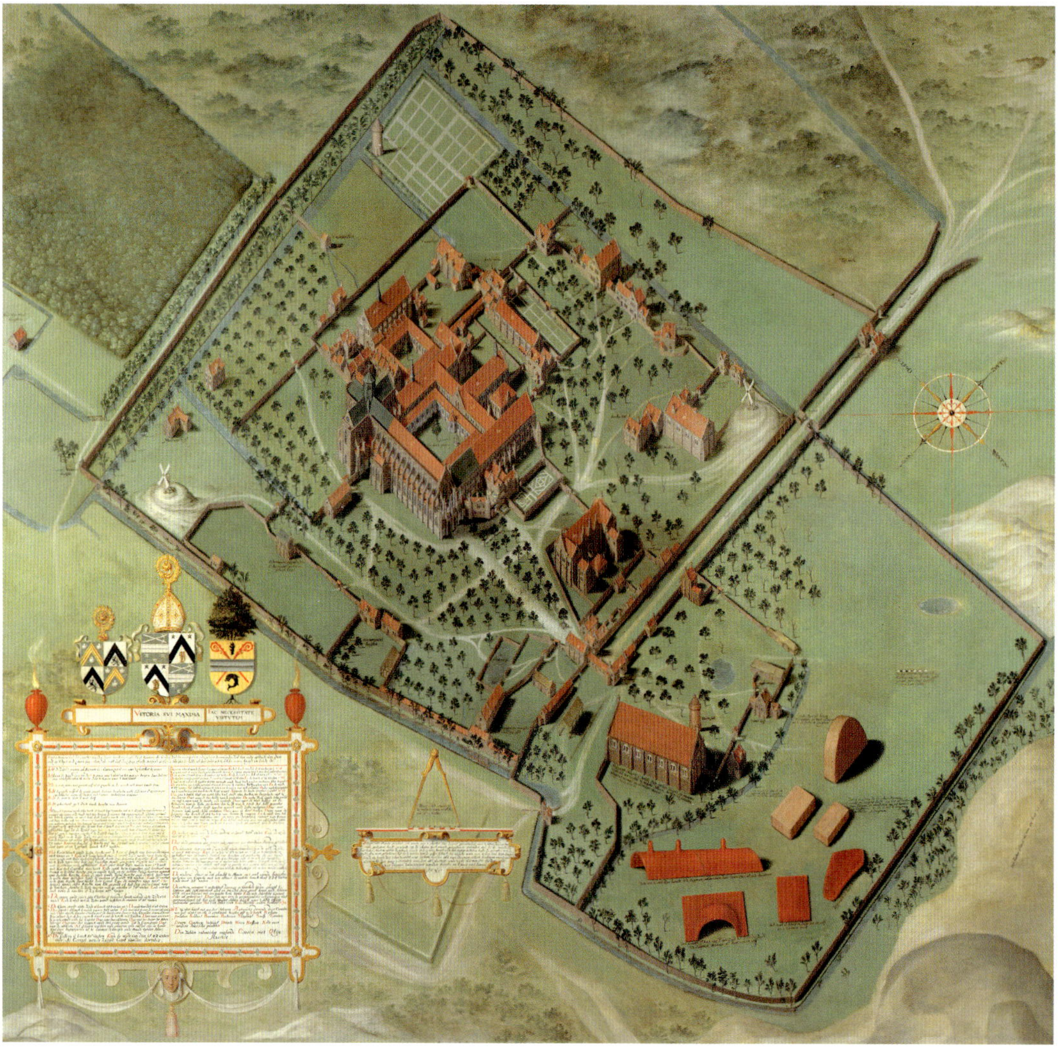

Fig. 56. Cistercian abbey of Ten Duinen (Belgium), enclosed microcosm subdivided into specialised areas, painting by Pieter Pourbus, 1556.
[Stedelijke Musea Brugge, © Lukas – Art in Flanders / photo Hugo Maertens]

occupants.[133] [Fig. 58] The Council of Trent (1545-63) set strict standards of enclosure for nuns and reduced their autonomy by subjecting them to the authority of bishops and the control of confessors. The reform of the Order of the Carmelite Women by Saint Teresa of Ávila († 1582) was one of the strictest applications of the 'Tridentine enclosure'.[134] Iron railings, double locked doors, peepholes and hatches were the only contact points with the outside

133 Jäggi and Lobbedey, 'Kirche und Klausur'; *Les dominicaines d'Unterlinden.*
134 Alford and De la Croix, 'L'ordre du Carmel'.

Fig. 57. Trappist Abbey of Westmalle (Belgium): rational layout made of concentric square enclosures including the church and the monastic buildings around the cloister, agricultural and industrial buildings, perspective drawing circa 1900.
[© KADOC, Leuven]

world. [Fig. 59] In this respect, the Second Vatican Council (1962-65) was for many religious houses a liberation from the practices of claustration inherited from the seventeenth and nineteenth centuries.

In the context of historical, architectural and archaeological studies, gender has long been used to compare the success of communities of monks and nuns, rather than as a criterion of specificity.

> To a great extent, the architecture of nunneries was based on standard monastic forms. But the forms varied from male houses in their arrangement, construction and development. Nunnery cloisters developed slowly, and often constituted of little more than a penticed walkway. (...) Nunneries were established for different purposes than monasteries by a different social group, largely the gentry, and were modelled on different prototypes, particularly those drawn from gentry settlements. (...) Perhaps nunneries never achieved economic prosperity because they were not intended to do so? (...) It seems that nunneries were founded in order to interact closely with the local community. It would seem then that medieval female religious experience was

Fig. 58. Beguinage of Bruges (Belgium), surrounded with a ditch, accessible from a bridge leading to the gatehouse dated 1776. The statue of Saint Elizabeth above the door and the inscription 'sauve garde' (safeguard) protect the beguinage from the evil.
[© THOC]

> *different* from that of men, not *less successful.* It has previously been misunderstood because it has been judged according to standards defined by male monasticism. (...)
> Monastic architecture was central to the social construction of difference between medieval religious men and women. Religious identities, personal mobility and perceptions of sexuality were maintained through space, boundaries and architectural embellishment. (...) Sexual segregation in monasteries and the greater enclosure of monastic women was in keeping with the lives which secular women of the 'inner household' lived in manor houses and castles.[135]

This social construction of the difference between men and women established by Roberta Gilchrist for the Middle Ages can undoubtedly be extrapolated for more recent times, in particular the seventeenth and nineteenth centuries. For example, the Beguines of the seventeenth and eighteenth centuries had local and modest origins, little or no education and maintained close links with female members of their families.[136] It was not uncommon for the widowed mother or sister of a Beguine to move into the beguinage.

135 Gilchrist, *Gender and Material Culture*, 190-192.
136 Coomans and Bergmans, *In zuiverheid leven*, 26-58.

Fig. 59. Monastery of the Augustine sisters of Québec (Canada) founded in 1639, main entrance to the enclosure: doorway (middle), peephole with grill and letterbox (right), foundling wheel or 'baby hatch' (left). [© THOC]

The Church has never been fond of 'double monasteries', monasteries in which distinct groups of monks and nuns live in a single community. Of course, it was not a question of mixed communities, but the formulas were varied, ranging from sharing the same rule, superior and heritage to a simple symbiosis between two neighbouring communities. Until the twelfth century, double foundations were numerous but all eventually evolved towards single communities because their functioning was problematic.[137] The most famous case was that of the order of Fontevraud, founded in 1101 by Robert of Arbrissel († 1116), whose double community was run by a noble abbess until the French Revolution. After the Counter-Reformation, and through the puritan nineteenth century, the Church remained uncompromising on the separation of genders and the impermeability of enclosures. Since the Second Vatican Council, some experiments with double communities have been carried out. The Monastic Fraternities of Jerusalem, founded by Pierre-Marie Delfieux in 1975, live the spirit of the monastic desert in the heart of cities. These distinct urban communities of monks, nuns and lay people celebrate offices together.

Before the Second Vatican Council, in communities of contemplative nuns, it was not uncommon for iron grills to separate the nuns' choir from the area accessible to the priest and the laity. A physical barrier symbolic of the enclosure, grills and bars could also be found in the gate house, parlours, sacristy and other points of potential contact with people who were not part of the community. Wheel hatches allowed for the transfer of objects from one space to another without seeing or being able to touch the other person. Some nunneries that took in abandoned children had a foundling wheel (baby hatch) that guaranteed both anonymity and the enclosure. [Fig. 59]

Inside the church or chapel, the enclosure also marked out liturgical provisions. The space of the monastic choir for monks and nuns was not accessible in principle to the laity, certainly not those of another sex. In nunneries of contemplative nuns subject to a strict enclosure, different forms of spatial organisation gave rise to particular architectural types. Often the nuns' choir with stalls was not at ground level but raised on a tribune. The laity admitted to the church had to remain below the tribune and could hear the nuns praying but could not see them. There were also L-shaped churches made of two naves joined at right angles. The nuns were in one nave and the laity had access to the other, with the altar positioned at the intersection of the two naves. [Fig. 60] Thus the two groups could face the altar but were not able to see each other. These particular arrangements linked to the enclosure explain why the layout in many monasteries can seem illogical. In fact, this sometimes complex layout was needed to prevent certain people from coming across one another.

137 Elm and Parisse, *Doppelklöster*.

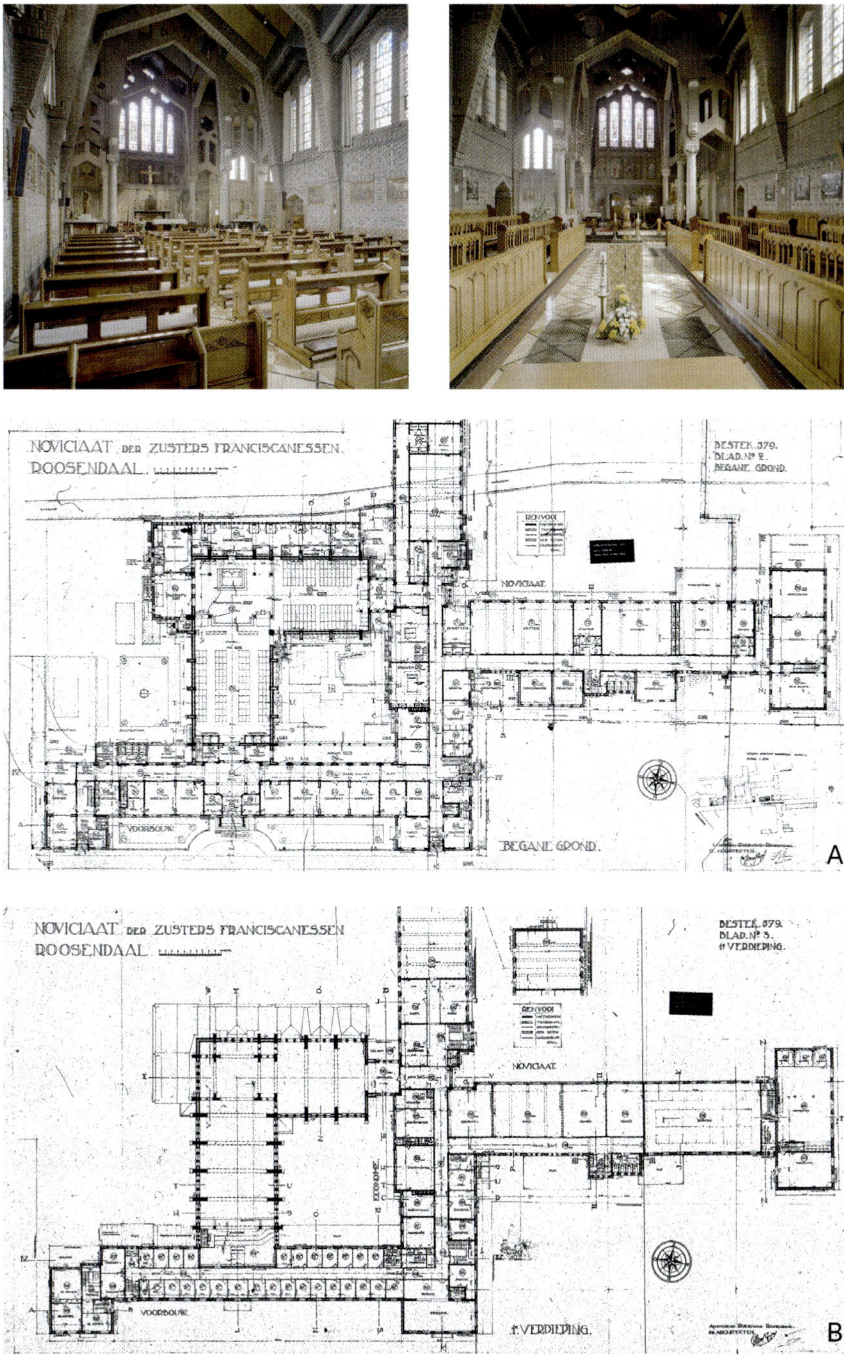

Fig. 60. L-shaped church of the Franciscan nunnery and novitiate of Mariadal in Roosendaal (The Netherlands), designed by Joseph Cuypers and Franciscus Sturm in 1934: views to the altar from the lay nave and nuns' choir, plans of the lower floor (A) and upper floor (B).
[© Rijksdienst voor het Cultureel Erfgoed, Amersfoort]

17. Liturgy and Identity

> The liturgy 'which appears to the public to be an esoteric discipline, or at least one of secondary interest, is in fact of capital importance in a community of monks or cannons as it governs their entire life and gives every order its own character. Calendar, ceremonial, rights, gestures and use of chanting; we should follow its entire development by period.'[138]

The liturgy varies according to orders, periods and even religious houses. In fact, whether contemplative or active, male or female, every order or religious institute, past or present, has specific liturgical features and an adapted schedule that depends first and foremost on the liturgy of the hours [see Chapter 4]. Not all have offices and the number of daily offices is not the same at every abbey, chanting does not play the same role everywhere and processions and devotions vary. The divine office only develops fully in contemplative communities, like the Benedictines and the Trappists, who give their liturgy an aesthetic dimension based on the relationship between the beautiful and the sacred. Many non-monastic orders replaced community offices in the choir of the church with individual reading of the breviary.

Form and background, material and immaterial – in a spiritual, aesthetic and sacred dimension – met and became intertwined more in the liturgy than anywhere else in religious community life. The liturgy necessarily has consequences on architecture because it takes place in a space. In fact, if architecture structures monastic space, it is liturgy that orders monastic time. In both cases, the cloister occupies the central place because it is used to go from one place to another, alone or in a procession, in silence, to go to work, prayer, the refectory, the chapter house or the dormitory. [Fig. 1] From the Middle Ages to the present, liturgy and its rituals have varied from one religious order to another and differed between communities of men and women.[139]

The liturgy also had a considerable influence on the architecture of monastery churches. The location of the monastic choir with stalls was and still is a constituent part of the morphology of the church. [Fig. 61] The choir could be located beneath the crossing, in the nave, at an elevated level (tribune), in the apse (beyond the altar), or at a right angle to the nave accessible to the laity. Without a contextual understanding of the liturgy, it is impossible to understand the layout and organisation of a monastery, abbey or convent.[140] The gender dimension of liturgy is not only related to the location of the choir in the church [see Chapter 16]. Because women could not become priests, they were not allowed to enter the sanctuary, approach the altar or the tabernacle.

138 Le Bras, 'Les Chartreux', 596.
139 Muschiol, 'Time and Space: Liturgy and Rite in Female Monasteries'.
140 Frommel and Lecomte, *La place du chœur.*

Fig. 61. Trappist abbey of Scourmont in Forges-les-Chimay (Belgium), liturgical arrangement of the monastic choir with tabernacle, high altar, stalls and lectern.
[© THOC]

Until the Second Vatican Council, these most sacred liturgical spaces were only accessible to religious men.

Although the liturgy was one of the pillars of monastic tradition, this does not mean that it was immutable. It was enriched with nuances and the successive touches of the men and women who made up the community. Reforms occasionally intervened, resulting in an in-depth reconsideration of the liturgy. The 'liturgical movement' – initiated by Dom Prosper Guéranger († 1875) and the Benedictines of Solesmes and continued under the aegis of Dom Lambert Beauduin († 1960) by the Benedictines of Mont César in Leuven – culminated in the liturgical changes decided at the Second Vatican Council in 1963.[141] These changes were: the partial abandonment of Latin in favour of vernacular languages, including during offices; the suppression of the difference between fathers and brothers or between mothers and sisters within communities; the abandonment of certain customs of dress; the modulation of silence; the simplification of many rituals, the meaning of which was no longer understood; the redefinition of the enclosure including in the church, etc. These changes were implemented and experienced differently according to the orders and places. Some inevitably caused tensions in the communities and had major consequences on spatial and architectural organisation. Inside the church, the relocation of the high altar and the possibility of concelebration gave rise to shifts that affected the very essence of monastic life: the divine office.

141 Nocent, *Le renouveau liturgique*.

18. Death and Memory

Death is always present in the minds of members of religious communities, but in a way that varies greatly. For Christians, death gives meaning to life, in the image of Christ dying on the cross and risen at Easter. This is especially true for members of religious communities who live with the expectation of encountering the Heavenly Jerusalem and the glorious return of Christ (*parousia*). The contemplative mystical nun is waiting for death that will put an end to her pilgrimage to earth and finally bring her to Christ, her mystical husband. [Fig. 62] Hospitaller brothers and sisters, faced with the suffering and death of men, women and children, carry out works of charity in the name of the Passion of Christ and love for one's neighbour. Finally, the desert and contemplative enclosure of the cloister can be seen as a sort of voluntary 'social death' in relation to the world and the temporal realm.

It is therefore not surprising that an abbey should be structured by a genuine topography of life and death, reminding the community of the meaning of life as a Christian, as well as the memory of its dead members.[142] Even the orientation of the chevet of the church towards the east is a manifestation of the axis of life and death. Every day, sunrise during the office of lauds is a reminder of the victory of light over darkness, of life over death [see Chapter 4].

In a monastery, death is also linked to the memory of the community. The book of the dead (*necrologium*) is a calendar-like book that remembered the birthdays of deceased monks or nuns; every day, the community would remember the dead of that particular day. Parts of a monastery were also visited by death, in particular the infirmary – where members would die and go to 'meet God' –, the church and places of burial. The location of the cemetery varied: often to the east or north of the church (abbeys) [Fig. 63], it was sometimes around the church when this was isolated (beguinages), in the middle of the cloister (Carthusians), or in undercrofts beneath the church (urban friaries, Jesuits). In addition, abbots and abbesses were buried in the chapter house during the Middle Ages, then in the church. [Fig. 64]

Members of the community who died in an 'odour of sanctity' were buried in the church and became objects of devotion, if not of worship. The majority of abbey churches built prior to the twelfth century have a crypt to which pilgrims would come to venerate relics of saints. A crypt is a subterranean vaulted space located beneath the church's sanctuary, intended to receive the tombs of holy people and play host to, even stimulate, their devotion by pilgrims. [Fig. 65] Depending on the success of pilgrimages, these crypts were subject to major architectural developments, including chapels and secondary altars.[143] [Fig. 11]

142 Cassidy-Welch, *Monastic Spaces and their Meanings*, 217-241.
143 Sapin, *Les cryptes en France*.

Fig. 62. Cistercian nunnery of Port-Royal des Champs (France): burial of a sister in the cloister, after Louise-Magdeleine Horthemels, circa 1710.
[© Musée de Port-Royal des Champs, Magny-les-Hameaux / photo RMN-Grand Palais, Gérard Blot]

Death had always been a source of income according to the well-known principle of exchange: 'I give you that you may give me' (*do ut des*).[144] The laity have always paid to be buried in monasteries or, when that was not possible, to obtain prayers of intercession. All dynasties founded funerary abbeys, sometimes even royal necropolises, such as that of the Habsburgs of Spain at El Escorial [see Chapter 13].[145] In order to secure their memory, princes

144 Bijsterveld, *Do ut des*.

145 Other dynastic necropolises are those of the kings of France at the Benedictine abbey of Saint Denis, the kings of Aragon at the Cistercian abbey of Poblet, the kings of Castile at the Cistercian abbey of Las Huelgas in Burgos, the kings of Portugal at the Cistercian abbey of Alcobaça and the Dominican abbey of Batalha, the Plantagenets at the abbey of Fontevraud, the kings of England at the Benedictine abbey of Westminster in London, the dukes of Burgundy at the Chartreuse of Champmol in Dijon, or the doges at the Dominicans in Venice, the emperors of Austria at the Capuchin friary in Vienna, etc.

Fig. 63. Trappist abbey of Koningshoeven (The Netherlands), founded in 1881, cemetery located east of the church.
[© THOC]

commissioned sumptuous tombs and richly endowed communities who were to pray for their salvation. [Fig. 31]

Beginning in the thirteenth century, mendicant orders offered burial possibilities to urban patrician families and by doing so secured an income, yet this also brought them into conflict with parishes who wanted the same burials for themselves.[146] Archaeological studies of burials in monastic cemeteries shed light on social identities and funerary rituals.[147] Architecture was organised to offer maximum burial possibilities, as shown by the excavation plan of the Franciscan church in London, in which tombs covered the ground without any spare space. [Fig. 66] Since the late eighteenth century and the introduction of cemetery legislation, burial inside parish and monastic churches has been gradually forbidden, with a handful of exceptions.

146 Bruzelius, *Preaching, Building, and Burying.*
147 Gilchrist and Sloane, *Requiem: The Medieval Monastic Cemetery in Britain.*

Fig. 64. Ruins of the Cistercian abbey of Jervaulx (England), tomb slabs of abbots in the chapter house, late twelfth century.
[© THOC]

19. Scale and Growth

Scale is a constituent character of monastic architecture; it varies considerably and is not necessarily in keeping with the size of the community. There is, in fact, little connection between the poor foundations of the Franciscan Third Order and the great royal foundations or Baroque German abbeys [see Chapter 13]. The degree of sanctity and virtue of a community is not measured by the scale of its buildings and it is no coincidence that many reforms came into being precisely as a result of excesses of grandeur. The conflict between Cluny and Cîteaux in the twelfth century is the best example of this.[148]

The scale of a monastery is the result of numerous factors, the primary of these being the income of the community. Abbeys with modest endowments were unable to 'think big' and develop because they did not have the means to support a large community or to diversify their patrimony in order to resist economic crises. The appearance in the late fifteenth century of commendatory abbots who appropriated a large part of the income for themselves condemned most of these abbeys to stagnate. Urban religious houses were deprived of landed property and dependent principally on the generosity of their benefactors, which could dry up or be transferred to other monasteries.

148 Birkedal Bruun, *Cambridge Companion on the Cistercian Order*, 25-37.

Fig. 65. Crypt of the Benedictine nunnery of Jouarre (France), established circa 680. [wikimedia.com]

Female nunneries and convents have always been smaller than male abbeys and monasteries because they were 'introverted' due to a stricter enclosure [see Chapter 16] and endowed with less property. Despite the obvious difference of social origin and architectural style between the Augustinian canonesses of the English Convent in Bruges and the Poor Clares in the neighbouring city of Roubaix, the scale of both nunneries is comparable. [Fig. 67 and 68]

If we take the cloister as a reference, we can see that the smallest were no more than 20 m long with a surface area of some 400 m^2, while the largest exceeded 50 m long, with a surface area of more than 2500 m^2, and were doubled by an upper floor. [Figs 16, 28 and 69] Knowing the role played by the cloister in a monk's daily life [see Chapter 5] it is possible to understand the influence of scale on his psychology and identity, ranging from humility and poverty to prestige and comfort. [Figs 1, 17 and 103]

The motherhouses of centralised orders were special religious houses because they concentrated a maximum of identity prestige, especially when they were home to the tomb of their founder or foundress and as such were places of pilgrimage: Saint Benedict at Monte Cassino, Saint Bernard at Clairvaux, Saint Francis in Assisi, Saint Dominic in Bologna, Saint Ignatius at the Gesù in Rome, Saint Angela Merici in Brescia, and so on. The greatest minds

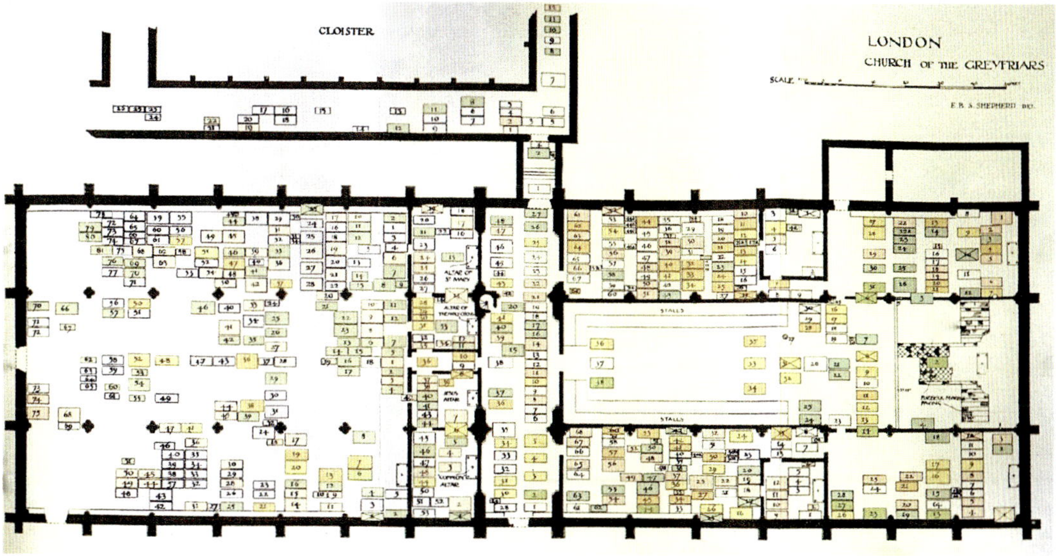

Fig. 66. Church of the Grey Friars or Franciscans in London (England), excavation plan showing the location of medieval burials.
[Shepherd, *Archaeological Journal*, 1902]

of the order usually lived in the motherhouses, which were also home to the order's administration and therefore required specific buildings such as archives, offices, libraries, meeting rooms and reception facilities.[149] Specialist houses for training, seminaries and other retreat centres developed their own architecture and opted for inspiring sites. The majority of international orders, congregations and religious institutes also built monasteries and other central houses in Rome. Finally, the motherhouses and regional hubs of missionary congregations and institutes, established in the capitals of colonial empires such as Lisbon, Madrid, Mexico and Goa, competed with one another for prestige.[150]

At the other end of the scale, the smallest religious houses hosted communities of twelve monks or nuns – a reference to the twelve apostles of Christ – or fewer. Some of these communities were not expected to remain at this size, while others were not expected to grow because their apostolate was small-scale. A typical example is the nineteenth-century Catholic parish school in rural area, which was run by three or four nuns and provided a traditional Catholic education at a local level. Such schools proliferated in the context of the First School War in Belgium (1879-84) thanks to sponsorship from the wealthy Catholic elite that fought to guarantee free education as

149 For instance, the motherhouse of the Cistercians: Plouvier and Saint-Denis, *Pour une histoire monumentale de l'abbaye de Cîteaux*.

150 About Lisbon: Henriques, Silva and Mégre, eds, 'Da Cidade Sacra à Cidade Laica'; LxConventos, <http://lxconventos.cm-lisboa.pt/> [accessed 20 July 2017].

Fig. 67. English Convent of the Augustinian canonesses in Bruges (Belgium), eighteenth-century corridor along the cloister.
[© THOC]
Fig. 68. Convent of the Poor Clares in Roubaix (France), designed by Jean-Baptiste Bethune in 1859.
[© THOC]

an alternative to the secular public education promoted by the Liberals. The archetypal Catholic village of Vivenkapelle near Bruges, designed by architects Jean-Baptiste Bethune and Florimond Van de Poele in 1861-67, consisted of a parish church, presbytery, a boys' primary school run by brothers and a girls' primary school run by sisters, all designed in Puginesque Gothic Revival style.[151] The enclosed girls' school has a very small inner courtyard or cloister. The nuns' convent is turned inwards around the cloister, while the classrooms developed to the north around the school's courtyard. [Fig. 70]

Among the characters of monastic architecture, it seems necessary to distinguish scale from growth. The latter is a process of the successive enlargement of space over time. Archaeologists and architectural historians study phases of growth, the complexity of which reflects historical density, ambitions and failures, and adaptations to changing circumstances. Four major growth processes can be defined.

The first is a process of centrifugal growth, starting from the cloister, which has already been mentioned in connection with Cluny II and Cluny III [see Chapter 6] and which is clearly illustrated, for example, by the plan of the Cistercian abbey of Tintern. [Fig. 71] The cloister was the centre from which the

151 Devliegher and Van Biervliet, 'Vivenkapelle. Een neogotisch kerkdorp'.

Fig. 69. Saint Hugh's Charterhouse, Parkminster (England), huge Gothic Revival complex with 34 hermitage houses, built in 1876-83 by architect Clovis Normand.
[© Commission Air / Alamy Stock Photo]

buildings extended out in all directions, including height. [Fig. 72] The principle of the centrifugal growth of a monastic complex was based on an obvious functional necessity: while work was being carried out, the daily life of the community had to be disrupted as little as possible. Work thus proceeded in successive stages and extensions depended on need and ended up no longer responding to a pre-established overall plan. In this respect, the morphology of Cluny II was much more planned than that of Cluny III, which resulted from unprecedented and unequalled growth. [Fig. 19]

The second process is that of the multiplication of cloisters and rectangular courtyards according to a grid system. Unlike the exceptional case of El Escorial, which was designed on a chessboard plan and built in a single phase [Fig. 42], it was not uncommon for abbeys to be extended by the addition of a second, or more rarely even a third cloister, according to a regular orthogonal pattern but one that was not originally anticipated. It was therefore the regularity of the base outline that determined the regularity of the extensions. One fascinating case is that of the Abbey of Tomar in Portugal, founded by the Knight Templars in the twelfth century and revived in the fourteenth century by a Portuguese military order, the Order of Christ, which made it its principal

Fig. 70. Primary girls' school and convent of Sisters of the Immaculate Conception in Vivenkapelle (Belgium), built in 1869 by architect Florimond Van de Poele. Ground floor: 1. entrance hall of the convent, 2. parlour, 3. chapel, 4. dining room, 5. kitchen, 6. common room, 7. storage , 8. small cloister, 9. service entrance, 10. entrance of the school, 11. staircase and hall, 12. classroom, 13. storage, 14. courtyard, 15. covered gallery. Upper floor: 16. study room, 17. cell, 18. common room, 19. polyvalent room.
[© Tine Neskens 2018. Photo © THOC]
convent school courtyard garden roof

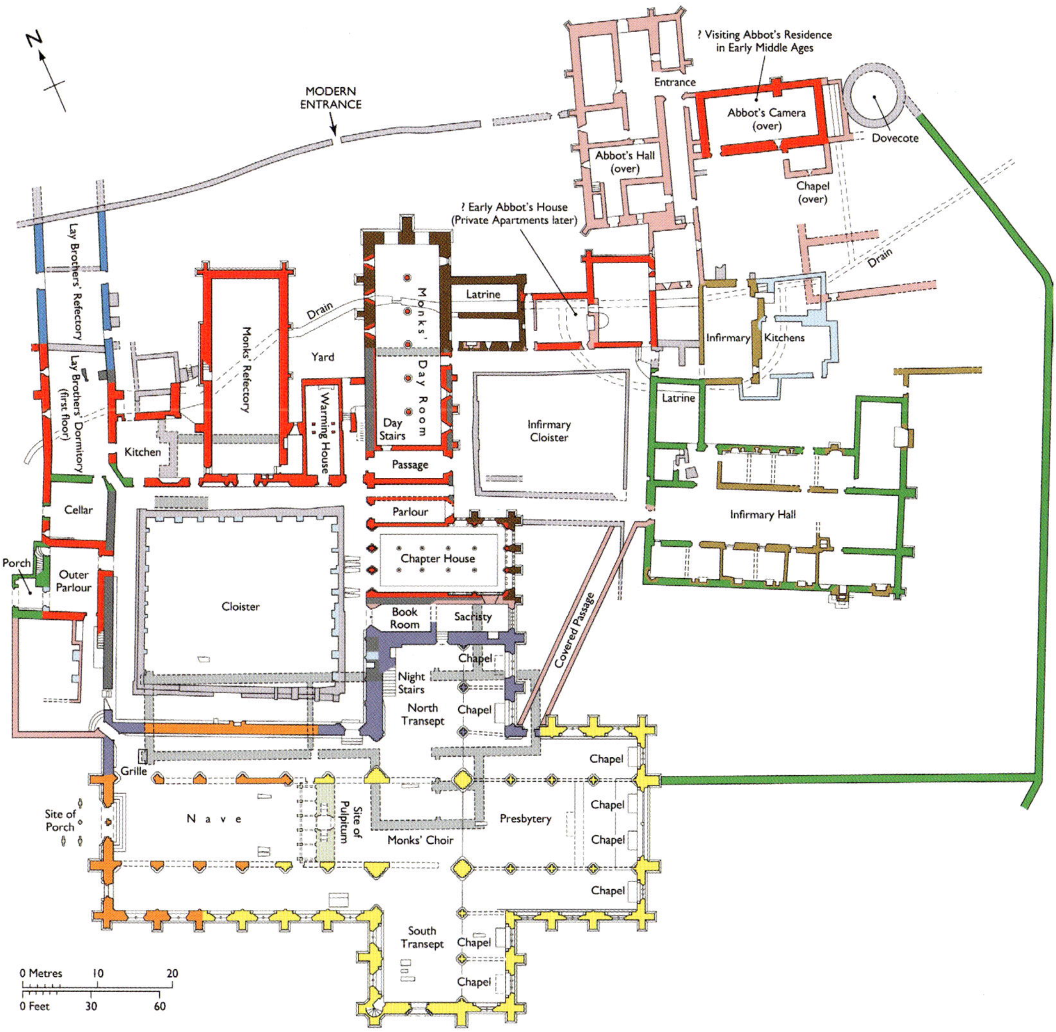

Fig. 71. Ground plan of the ruined Cistercian abbey of Tintern (Wales): the buildings' chronology shows the growth of the complex; the comparison of the small twelfth-century Romanesque church (grey) and the large late thirteenth-century Gothic church (light blue) illustrates the change of scale.
[© Crown copyright (2017) Cadw, Welsh Government]

- upstanding walls / visible foundations
- buried / lost walls

First stone monastery
- 12th century (upstanding)
- 12th century (buried)

Late 12th to 13th century
- phase I (late 12th to early 13th century)
- phase II (centred on 1232-45)
- phase III (?)
- phase IV (mid- to late 13th century)

The Gothic church (about 1269 to 1330)
- phase I (about 1269 to 1288)
- phase II (completed about 1288-1301+)
- phase III (completed about 1288-1301+)
- phase IV (about 1320-30)

The Later Middle Ages
- 14th century
- 15th century (? earlier)
- 15th century (? later)
- uncertain / modern

Fig. 72. Premonstratensian abbey of Park in Leuven (Belgium) founded in 1129, cloister garth surrounded by buildings from the twelfth to the eighteenth century.
[© THOC]

base for colonial expansion from the fifteenth century. [Fig. 28] The means available were considerable and no fewer than seven cloisters were built between the twelfth and eighteenth centuries in different styles, including the cloister of Don João III, a pure Renaissance masterpiece (1557-91).

The third process of growth is that of the 'clean slate', which consisted of building a brand new abbey on the site of an old one. Many abbeys, in particular the Baroque abbeys of Bavaria and Austria, were rebuilt in the eighteenth century on regular plans that looked like palaces [see Chapter 13]. The church was often retained but converted to the taste of the day, and medieval building foundations were reused to save time and money. It was much more unusual for a new abbey to be built on the site of an old one with a completely different plan. [Fig. 45] At the Benedictine abbeys of Ottobeuren (Baroque) and Sankt-Blasien (neo-classical), there was nothing left of the medieval abbey: building layout, scale and even the turning of the church axis demonstrated the extent to which the community rejected the past and opted for a project of unprecedented prestige, with demonstrative façades and domed churches staged in the most theatrical way possible in a grandiose landscape.

The fourth process is that of the re-foundation of an abbey on an abandoned and ruined site that retained the ruin of the former abbey as a material relic and evidence of a long spiritual tradition. This scenario involved a break

Fig. 73. Trappist abbey of Orval (Belgium) rebuilt by architect Henry Vaes in 1926-48 on the foundations of the destroyed eighteenth-century abbey, near the ruins of the medieval abbey.
[© Aerial photos.com / Alamy Stock Photo]

followed by a re-foundation [see Chapter 15]. More than a romantic approach, it was the power of the attraction of the site and an awareness of history and heritage that were at work here. Building the future alongside ruins is the exact opposite of a clean slate. The Trappist abbey of Orval was rebuilt between 1926 and 1948 alongside the ruins of the medieval abbey and on the foundations of the eighteenth-century abbey that had been destroyed during the French Revolution. Comparing the scale and style of the medieval ruins and the triumphant neo-Romanesque abbey speaks volumes as to the ambitions and significance of the new foundation on the old site.[152] [Fig. 73]

It was not uncommon for megalomaniac projects to remain unfinished: here, a church limited to just its lower storeys – like the choir of the Dominican monastery of Batalha – there, a nave ending in a temporary wall awaiting a façade – like the Premonstratensian church in Grimbergen or the church of the Dominican friary in Saint-Maximin [Fig. 74] – not to mention the many stunted towers. This incompleteness would become a part of the identity of the monastery, not without leading to frustrations. Some refer to the existence of a 'culture of incompleteness', which was thought to help mobilise the community when it came to generating donations, much like the building sites of cathedrals.

152 Soetens, *Orval 1926-1948*.

Fig. 74. Saint Magdalene's Church of the Dominican friary in Saint-Maximin (France), incomplete façade after works stopped in 1532.
[© THOC]

Be that as it may, the present state of an abbey is the result of centuries of construction, of which it is difficult to reconstruct all the intermediate states. These 'palimpsest abbeys' were nevertheless experienced on a day-to-day basis by successive generations of monks and nuns. [Fig. 71] This phenomenon only occurs in the presence of buildings that clearly demonstrate these breaks in architecture, scale, form, colours, materials and, of course, style. For the community of the Benedictine abbey on Reichenau Island, the construction of a high polygonal Gothic apse in place of a straight Romanesque chevet must have been a veritable aesthetic revolution, which accompanied a change in the liturgy and no doubt deeper reform. The contrasts between classical and Gothic architecture at the Benedictine abbey of Bec-Hellouin, or between classical and neo-Gothic architecture at the Benedictine abbey of Solesmes [Fig. 75], also carry meaning and are the result of precise historical contexts. In their time, these contrasts were probably as violent as those of the 1960s between the modernity promoted by the Second Vatican Council and the revival styles of the nineteenth century.

Fig. 75. Benedictine abbey of Saint Peter's of Solesmes (France): classical building from 1722, remains of the former priory suppressed during the French Revolution, and Gothic Revival wing from 1896, built after the re-establishment of the abbey in 1833 by Dom Prosper Guéranger.
[© robertharding/Alamy Stock Photo].

20. Style

Style is the character most often mentioned by art historians and monastery guides because it is both clear to see and carries with it the building's identity. It is indeed the case that Cluniacs are commonly associated with Romanesque art, Cistercians with a rejection of decoration, mendicant orders with pared-down Gothic structures, Jesuits with the Baroque, Bavarian and Austrian Benedictines with late Baroque and Rococo [Fig. 76], other Benedictines with Gothic Revival, and Dominicans with modern art. Such stereotypes are facile and reductive. Why, for example, did the Premonstratensians of Floreffe convert the interior of the Romanesque abbey completely to the neo-classical style in 1770?[153] Why did the Jesuits of Brussels build the monumental church of their new college in 1908-12 in a medieval style (Rhenish neo-Romanesque, with a westwork) despite the lack of any historical connection with the Roman and Baroque identity of the Society of Jesus?[154] [Fig. 46] Every order and community experienced internal debates when faced with difficult choices linked to architectural projects. In fact, these projects were mostly linked to foundations or reforms, and changing meant altering tradition. This lies at the

153 *L'ancienne abbaye de Floreffe 1121-1996*.
154 Coomans, 'L'église Saint-Jean-Berchmans du Collège Saint-Michel'.

Fig. 76. Library of the Benedictine abbey of Saint Gall (Switzerland), rebuilt by Peter Thumb in 1758-67. [© Prisma by Dukas Presseagentur/Alamy Stock Photo]

heart of the question of relationships between tradition and modernity that constitute the very essence of the dynamic of a society or group, including a religious community.

There is no need here to draw up the catalogue of styles and their chronological and regional variations established and debated by art historians; instead we will focus on two points related to the issue of style. First and foremost, the relativity of modernity, a notion that is overused if ever there was one, as modernity is always established in relation to something else. It can be said that Gothic was modern in relation to Romanesque, Baroque to Gothic and even Gothic Revival to classical, etc.[155] The anonymous master builder of the Basilica of Saint Francis in Assisi and Giacomo Vignola, the architect of the Gesù church of the Jesuits in Rome, were both modern despite belonging to diametrically opposed architectural traditions, one medieval and the other classical. Their harmonic systems and relations to ornament have little in common and the spaces they created inspired very different feelings. Like the characters already mentioned, style is important when it comes to decoding in order to contextualise and fully understand the meaning of the building and the project it expresses.

155 Trachtenberg, 'Reflections on "Gothic Architecture" as Medieval Modernism'.

Fig. 77. Saint Ignatius Loyola church of the Jesuits in Antwerp (Belgium), now Saint Charles Borromeo church, designed in the Baroque style by father François d'Aguilon and brother Pieter Huyssens, 1615-21. [© Oswald Pauwels]

The second question relating to style is that of the identity of the architects and their choices. If there was a Cistercian style, or more precisely, a way of building in conformity with the prescriptions of the Cistercian order, there must have been Cistercian master builders who were experts in it and responsible for its dissemination.[156] This question is a legacy of nineteenth-century historiography and is mirrored by the romantic figure of the 'monk-builder',[157] so prized in the context of the religious revival after the French Revolution and in debates about whether or not an architect had to be Christian to be able to build churches. There were certainly monks who were architects as well as architectural guidelines in every order. Stylistic identities, however, cannot be

156 Coomans, 'Cistercian architecture'; Untermann, *Forma Ordinis*.
157 Including the famous novel about Le Thoronet: Pouillon, *The Stones of the Abbey*.

Fig. 78. Jeronimós Monastery in Lisbon (Portugal), by architects Diogo Boitac and Juan de Castilho, early sixteenth century.
[© THOC].

reduced to the action of a few people or a few decorative characteristics, just as architectural design cannot be reduced to style and ornament.

Without doubt, the question of the monk-architect was also nurtured by the Jesuits and other seventeenth-century orders that had important and well organised building activities. The Society of Jesus had coadjutor brothers who were architects, whose plans were necessarily submitted for approval by the central authorities of the Jesuit Curia in Rome.[158] It was long believed that this form of censorship had forged a typical and identifying 'Jesuit style', but it should be noted that the central authorities insisted first and foremost on the adaptation of architecture to local conditions (integration), its suitability to the needs of the establishment (specificity), and the rejection of any form of financial borrowing to complete these constructions (autonomy). Every Jesuit province, in Europe and the colonies, had its great architects: brother Étienne Martellange († 1641) in France, brother Pieter Huyssens († 1633) and brother Jean du Blocq († 1656) in the Southern Low Countries, etc. [Fig. 77] Style as an instrument of propaganda and a bearer of Tridentine Catholic identity was highly present in Baroque art and architecture but was in no way specific to

158 Snaet, 'Fort the Greater Glory of God'; Lombaerde, *Innovation and Experience*; Álvaro Zamora, Ibáñez Fernández and Criado Mainar, *La arquitectura jesuítica*.

monastic milieux or to the Jesuits.[159] The stylistic uniformity of Jesuit architecture, in the same way as that of the Cistercians and the 'typical plans' of the Middle Ages, as well as that of other orders, has been greatly exaggerated.

The stylistic aspect of a monastery or religious house can result from four scenarios that bring with them meaning, history and identity. Firstly, some abbeys demonstrate a homogeneous style, either because they were built quickly and to an overall design or restored with the intention of (re)discovering a homogeneous identity. Secondly, other abbeys have a composite appearance, displaying a mixture of styles and periods, resulting from successive transformations over the passing of time. These complexes form valuable and venerable palimpsests [see Chapter 19]. Thirdly, some monasteries consist of two distinct styles, an expression of a conflicting relationship between two precise historical moments, likely linked to internal reforms. [Fig. 75] Fourthly, many religious houses with a more or less modern appearance do not show any precise style or ornamentation but express an intentional poverty, an intentional simplicity or just functional efficiency.

In the nineteenth century, the question of style took another turn when ambient historicism gave some occasionally surprising meanings to the use of specific styles. The great monastic orders that had been shaken like never before by the French Revolution sought to regain their foothold and were forced to build new abbeys. From a liturgical and archaeological perspective, with reference to an idealised Middle Ages, a fascinating neo-medievalism developed, fortunately illustrated by photographs that suggested that the monks themselves were neo-Gothic! [Fig. 22] The Trappist abbey of Mount St Bernard, designed by Augustus Welby Northmore Pugin in 1839,[160] the Benedictine abbey of Maredsous by Jean-Baptiste Béthune in 1872, the Abbey of La Grande-Trappe in Normandy by Alfred Tessier in 1887, the Charterhouse of Parkminster by Clovis Normand in 1876-83, and the Dominican monastery of Prouille in Fanjeaux, rebuilt in 1879, are based on an archaeological knowledge of medieval styles, a condition of 'true' and legitimate architecture. [Figs 69, 78 and 80] According to Pugin, Bethune and others, the Gothic style and the art of building had a Christian and moral dimension that contrasted profoundly with 'pagan' classical, 'bastardised' eclectic or industrial architecture. Gothic Revival became a reference style for many Catholic convents and monasteries, whose architectural style is not always remarkable but expresses a strong identity through the use of easily recognisable forms such as pointed arches, rose windows, pinnacles, spires, etc.

Founded in 1901, the Benedictine Saint Andrews Abbey of Zevenkerken in Bruges is unique.[161] This abbey has seven interlocking churches and chapels,

159 Bazin, *Les Palais de la Foi*.
160 Young, 'A.W.N. Pugin's Mount Saint Bernard Abbey'.
161 Papeians de Morchoven, *L'abbaye de Saint-André Zevenkerken*.

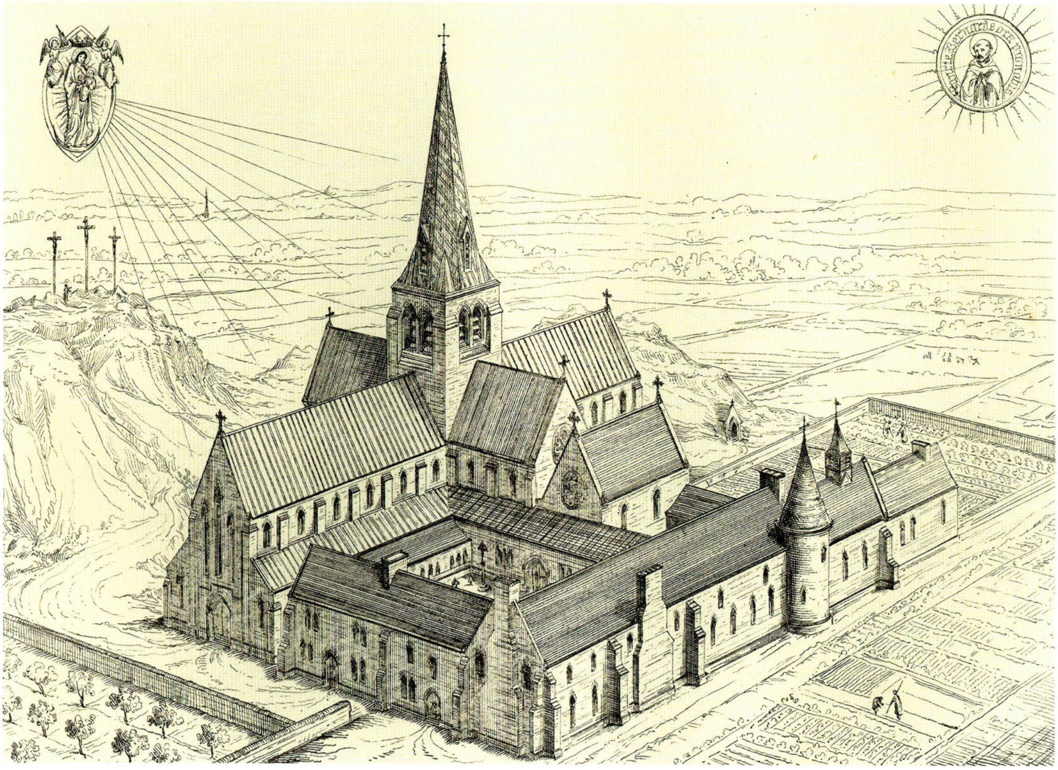

Fig. 79. Trappist abbey of Mount St Bernard (England), Gothic Revival design by Augustus Welby Pugin, 1839, published in T.H. King, *Les vrais principes de l'architecture ogivale ou chrétienne*, Bruges, 1850. [© KADOC, Leuven]

each in a different style: a Roman catacomb, early Christian, Romanesque, Byzantine, Gothic, Renaissance and Russian Orthodox. [Fig. 79] They symbolise the utopian synthesis and universality of the Roman Catholic Church in time and space. The number seven refers to the patriarchal basilicas of Rome and gives the abbey its name of 'seven churches' (*Zevenkerken*). This remarkable architectural complex was founded and supported by Rome as a training centre for Benedictine missionaries destined to evangelise Brasil, Congo and other countries. The style of the Benedictine abbey of Chevetogne, founded in 1929, expresses its original ecumenical design that combines the great traditions of liturgical prayer of the East and West. The abbey has two churches: one, for Latin rites, was inspired by early Christian basilicas; the other, for Byzantine rites, takes the form of a Greek cross. After the Second World War, the monastic community of Taizé developed another form of ecumenism by uniting brothers of different Christian confessions into a single community.

Equally fascinating is the way in which the twentieth century attempted to rid itself of the historicist revival styles of the previous century. Polychromy

Fig. 80. Cloister and church of the Gothic Revival Benedictine abbey of Maredsous (Belgium), designed by Jean-Baptiste Bethune, built in 1872-92.
[© THOC]

and neo-Gothic furniture disappeared in many abbeys in favour of whitewashing or sanding. Elsewhere, there were experiments with hybrid couplings, such as at the Benedictine abbey of Douai in Woolhampton, where, in the 1960s, a nave made from a metallic structure was built in front of the neo-Gothic choir. More recently still, a generation of post-modern monks in search of an otherwise authentic image,[162] embarked upon 'façadism', dressing a Gothic Revival church in Romanesque pastiche, as at the Trappist abbey of Rochefort, or by erecting a modern façade in front of a nineteenth-century one, such as at the Benedictine abbey of La-Pierre-qui-Vire. These cases illustrate just how essential architecture is for a community, even going so far as to provoke unease or even conflicts of identity.

In the *Apologia*, written in 1125, Saint Bernard expressed his opinion on the place of visual arts in the abbeys. He lashes out at the richness of churches and the bestiary of Romanesque capitals in cloisters:

> On vanity of vanities, yet no more vain than insane! The church is resplendent in her walls and wanting in her poor. She dresses her stones in gold and lets her sons go naked. The eyes of the rich are fed at the expense of the indigent. The curious find something to amuse them and the needy find nothing to sustain them. But in cloisters, where the brothers are reading, what is the point of this ridiculous monstrosity, this shapely misshapenness, this misshapen shapeliness? (...) In short, so many and so marvellous are the various shapes surrounding us that it is more pleasant to read the marble than the books, and to spend the whole day marvelling over these things rather than meditating on the law of God. Good Lord! If we aren't embarrassed by the silliness of it all, shouldn't we at least be disgusted by the expense? [163]

This spirit of strictness prevailed in the construction of Cistercian Romanesque cloisters, devoid of the colourful figurative representations and other distracting anecdotes that filled the Benedictine cloisters of Moissac, Cuxa, Silos, Ripoll and many more.[164] [Fig. 81] Twelfth-century Cistercian architecture was without ornament and found perfection in a relationship of proportions and pure forms, such as at the Abbey of Thoronet. The cloisters painted by Fra Angelico in Florence, the flamboyant cloister of the Jerónimos in Lisbon, and those of the Baroque abbeys in Bavaria and Austria [Fig. 43], for example, are light-years away from these Cistercian Romanesque abbeys [Fig. 50], and yet they all had the same function and the essence of monastic life within them was identical.

162 Jonvaux, 'Patrimonialisation des monastères'.
163 Bernard of Clairvaux, *Apologia*, Chapter 12, 28-29.
164 Cassanelli and Lopez-Tello Garcia, *Saint Benoît et son héritage artistique*; Vergnolle, *L'art roman en France*, 235-283.

Fig. 81. Benedictine abbey of Santo Domingo de Silos (Spain), cloister with rich Romanesque figurative sculpture, late eleventh and twelfth century.
[© Image Broker / Alamy Stock Photo]

Dom Hans van der Laan, designer of the extremely pared-down concrete architecture of the Abbey of Sint-Benedictusberg in Vaals [Fig. 12] and the nunnery of Roosenberg in Waasmunster [Fig. 25],[165] must undoubtedly have felt repulsed by the colourful architecture and brick corbels of his Benedictine predecessor Dom Paul Bellot († 1944),[166] who himself had freed himself from the Benedictine Gothic Revival of Solesmes and Maredsous [Figs 75 and 80], and the artistic tradition of the abbey school of Beuron. Yet they all belonged to the same Benedictine family and the same monastic tradition; only one generation separated these two monk-architects. One generation it may have been but what a generation it was! That of the 1950s and early 1960s, which anticipated the Second Vatican Council and, under the visionary impulse of the Dominicans Marie-Alain Couturier († 1954) and Pie Raymond Régamey († 1996), dared to promote a modern architecture and sacred art. The challenge lay in proposing fundamental changes to regenerate tradition without

165 Ferlenga and Verde, *Dom Hans van der Laan*; Padovan, *Dom Hans van der Laan*; Voet, *Dom Hans van der Laan*.

166 Culot and Méade, *Dom Bellot: moine-architecte*.

Fig. 82. Carmel de la Paix in Mazille (France), designed by Josep Lluís Sert, 1968-72. [Chabe01, Wikimedia Commons]

rejecting it, as well as renewing the relationship between the Church and a modern world in flux.

The church of the Benedictine abbey of St. John's in Collegeville (Minnesota) designed by Marcel Breuer and built from 1952 to 1961, the convent of La Tourette, the training centre for the Dominicans of Lyon in Eveux (France) designed by Le Corbusier and built from 1956 to 1960 [Fig. 83], the church of the Benedictine abbey of St. Mary and St. Louis (Missouri) designed by Gyo Obata (HOK) and built with the contribution of Pier Luigi Nervi in 1962, and the Carmel de la Paix in Mazille (France) designed by Josep Lluís Sert and built in 1968-72 [Fig. 82], are masterpieces of a generation of modernist architects who refused to reason in terms of 'architectural heritage'.[167] The 'house monasteries' of the late 1960s were part of the same movement [see Chapter 14]. These buildings prove that modernity went well beyond a question of style, but expressed a spirit inspired by faith in the future on the part of a generation traumatised by the Second World War. This generation was not mistaken, but it was not followed by what its impetus could have hoped for. The drying up of

167 Stehman, 'L'aventure du nouveau Saint-John's'; Henze, *La Tourette*; Birksted, *An Architecture of Ineloquence: José Lluis Sert's Carmel de la Paix.*

Fig. 83. Dominican Priory of Sainte Marie de La Tourette near Lyon (France), designed by Le Corbusier from 1953 and built in 1956-60.
[© THOC]

religious vocations in Western Europe since the late 1960s led to the transformation, adaptation and eventual closure of religious houses.

As the twenty-first century begins, the construction of a new monastery is a rather exceptional event and sometimes gives rise to architectural creations of remarkable quality, such as the Trappist abbeys of Nový Dvůr (Czech Republic), built in 2001-04 from plans by the architect John Pawson, and the Abbey Val Notre-Dame in Saint-Jean-de-Matha (Québec), after plans by the architect Pierre Thibault in 2007-09. Contemporary architectural vocabulary, materials and design are put at the service of centuries-old monastic traditions. The cloister remains at the centre of the monastery. In evolving urban contexts, small communities sometimes found new 'house-monasteries' such as the Dominican Convent of Fra Angelico built in 2007-09 in the university town of Louvain-la-Neuve. Its spirit remains close of that of the Dominican convent of Froidmont [see Chapter 14], but its architectural style is postmodern.

Fig. 84. Former Convento de São João Evangelista, Convento dos Lóios, in Évora (Portugal), now a hotel. [© THOC]

AFTERLIFE

ADAPTIVE REUSE AND HERITAGISATION

The fourth section of this book is devoted to other uses for monasteries. It is a reflection on a contemporary issue in Western Europe and North America. Beginning in the late 1960s, the drying up of religious vocations has resulted, half a century later, in a considerable loss of interest in convents, monasteries and other religious institutes. In recent decades, hundreds of urban and rural religious houses have been sold, destroyed, converted, reused and so on. Elsewhere, older monastic communities have merged; others are questioning the future of their heritage. In The Netherlands, for example, 172 'living' monasteries were counted in 2008. By simple demographic projection, it is expected that about 150 will have ceased their religious activity by 2020.[168] This gives an idea of the extent of the phenomenon that also affects France, Spain, Italy, Belgium, Ireland, Québec and other countries with a more conservative Catholic sociology.

Reuse of existing buildings and sites for other purposes than their initial use is an age-old practice. However, 'reuse', 'adaptation' and 'adaptive reuse' of historic buildings with the awareness of their heritage values and the cultural significance of the place, is a relatively recent phenomenon. It has been theorised in several international documents for heritage conservation and restoration issued by ICOMOS such as the Venice Charter in 1964 (article 5) and the Burra Charter in 2013 (article 21). Today, adaptive reuse deals with all

168 Nelissen, 'Convents in the Netherlands'.

building types and is evolving according to criteria including economy, sustainability, community life, education, etc.[169]

Contrary to what may be believed, the reuse of abbeys, monasteries and convents for purposes other than those for which they were designed is not a new phenomenon. In a previous publication, we demonstrated that there is a long tradition in this area.[170] Over roughly the last two centuries, the reuse of monasteries has taken on a heritage dimension that develops precisely when the object loses or has lost its use value.

In Europe, one thinks primarily of the secularisation of monasteries and the suppression of religious communities after the French Revolution, the redistribution of land and the massive destruction that ensued. Monasteries have always been coveted, for their real estate value in particular. In the countries that became Protestant in the sixteenth century, suppressed monasteries, friaries and convents were often demolished and the land subdivided, in particular in urban settings. In many cases, only a street name recalls their presence. This is true of Bruges, a supreme town of history, heritage, and numerous urban monasteries and convents. They were all suppressed in 1796 and many were demolished in the years that followed, including the four friaries built by the mendicant orders in the thirteenth century.[171] In the streets that now bear their names,[172] one would search in vain for the material remains of these buildings. [Fig. 85] An accurate study of the secularisation of the friary of the Carmelites in Brussels shows how new streets were established through the former enclosure, along two sides of the former church. Because of the favourable location of the grounds, new houses were rapidly built, some reusing the foundations of older buildings, and most visible traces of the friary quickly disappeared. [Fig. 86]

The abbeys, monasteries and convents suppressed in the sixteenth century or late eighteenth century but not destroyed owe their salvation to a combination of circumstances, as well as sufficiently sustainable new uses. The majority of Catholic hospitals and educational establishments retained their use but were secularised. For others, the quality of the places and the morphology of the buildings around the cloister favoured certain types of adaptive reuse, even before the issue became an explicitly heritage-focused one.

What follows offers a typology of other uses, from farm to museum and library, including factory, barracks, prison, school and other forms of housing. Some reuses were motivated only by pragmatic considerations devoid of any heritage dimension. This developed gradually and in a very variable way depending on the case.

169 Fiorani, Kealy and Musso, *Conservation – Adaptation*.

170 Coomans, 'Reuse of Sacred Places: Perspectives for a Long Tradition'.

171 Except remains of one wing of the Dominican convent. See: Coomans, 'L'architecture médiévale des ordres mendicants'.

172 Minderbroedersstraat, Predikherenrei, Augustijnenrei and Carmersstraat.

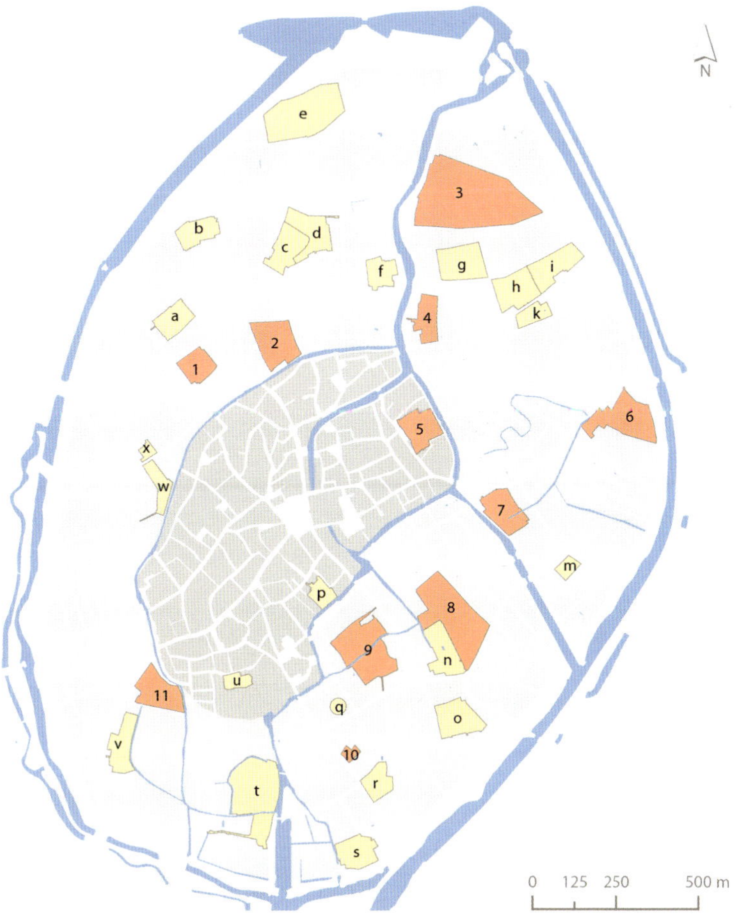

Fig. 85. Map of the city of Bruges (Belgium) at the end of the eighteenth century, with the location and identification of male and female religious houses, all of which were secularised in 1796.
[© Reinout Klaarenbeek]

- female convents
- male abbeys, friaries and monastries

Background

- area within the early 12th-century wall
- area within the late 13th-century wall
- water

Male orders

1. Discalced Carmelites
2. Augustinians
3. Cistercians, Dunes Abbey
4. Carmelites
5. Jesuits
6. Carthusians
7. Dominicans
8. Franciscans
9. Regular Canons, Eekhout Abbey
10. Alexians
11. Capuchins

Female orders

a. Discalced Carmelite sisters
b. Carmelite sisters 'Sion'
c. Cistercians nuns 'Hemelsdale'
d. Annuntiate sisters
e. Rich Clares
f. Regular Canonesses 'Sarepta'
g. Cistercians nuns 'Spermalie'
h. Regular Canonesses 'English convent'
i. Regular Canonesses 'Bethanien'
k. Franciscan grey sisters (1)
m. Apostolines
n. Regular Canonesses 'Saint Trudo'
o. Dominican sisters
p. Carthusian sisters
q. Franciscan black sisters
r. Capuchinesses
s. Poor Clares
t. Beguines
u. Franciscan sisters 'Conceptionalists'
v. Regular Canonesses 'Saint Godelieve'
w. Franciscan grey sisters (2)
x. Carmelites Maricols

Fig. 86. The medieval friary of Carmelites in Brussels (Belgium) completely disappeared from the cityscape in the decades that followed its suppression in 1796.
[© Reinout Klaarenbeek]

- boundary of the friary
- church
- buildings of the community
- garden
- built area
- boundary of the former friary
- new buildings along the street
- parcel boundary

'Heritagisation' is the process by which the awareness of the heritage values of an object is realised. Heritagisation teaches us as much about the people who have heritagised the object as about the heritage object itself.[173]

The typological discussion that follows is not exhaustive because reuses are in their thousands and they are all anchored in particular contexts. The specific literature on the reuse of monasteries and convents is much more limited than the literature on the reuse of churches and religious heritage in general.[174] This research topic will inevitably develop in the coming years because of the increasing number of reused religious houses. There will soon be a need for accurate critical evaluation of the adaptive reuse of former monasteries and religious houses, including economical, social, religious, maintenance, urbanistic and environmental aspects.

173 Morisset, 'Patrimony, the Concept, the Object, the Memory, and the Palimpsest'.
174 Noppen, Coomans and Drouin, *Des couvents en heritage / Religious Houses: A Legacy*; Adriaenssens, Booth and De Clus, *Converted Monasteries*; Henriques, Silva and Mégre, 'Da Cidade Sacra à Cidade Laica'.

21. Destruction and Ruins

At all times, the most violent suppressions of religious establishments have been accompanied by looting, destruction, exodus and massacres. The monastic memory, recorded in martyrologies and kept up through devotion to saints, includes many martyrs, from the time of the Desert Fathers to the Tibhirine massacre in 1996,[175] raids by the Huns and Vikings, Calvinist republics, missionary martyrs all over the world, the Spanish Civil War, and all wars that unleashed indiscriminate violence. We will not return here to the particular vocation of military orders or to the suppression of the Templars [see Chapter 8].

Other large-scale suppressions of religious establishments, decided by a sovereign or central authority, were carried out either with or without physical violence but led to the significant transfer of property and reuse: the abolition of all the abbeys in England by King Henry VIII in 1536-41, the suppression of the Society of Jesus by Pope Clement XIV in 1773, the suppression of contemplative religious orders found to be 'useless' by the enlightened Emperor Joseph II in Austria, Hungary and the Southern Low Countries in the 1780s (Josephinism), the sack of numerous religious establishments in France from 1789, and the suppression of hundreds of abbeys and monasteries in France and territories conquered by the French Republic by the Directory decree on 1 September 1796. The total number of suppressions has still to be accurately quantified.[176]

In the nineteenth century, lay governments used 'concordats' to regulate new relationships between the Church and State. However, these agreements concerned only diocesan structures and parishes, not monasteries or religious orders. Anticlerical governments also regularly lashed out at religious institutes and partial or total secularisations, accompanied by a new wave of expulsions, seizures and sales, took place in most European countries, and even beyond: in Portugal in 1834; the *desamortización* in Spain in 1836 and 1855; the *Sonderbund* in Switzerland in 1845; the *Kulturkampf* in West Prussia in 1871-80; the 'Ferry laws' and the 'Combes laws' in France in 1880-81 and 1901-04 respectively; not forgetting Communism in Russia from 1917 and in Central Europe from 1945 to 1989.[177] On each occasion, hundreds of communities were expelled and were forced to take refuge in countries whose constitutions guaranteed religious freedom and freedom of association, such as Belgium, The Netherlands, Switzerland, Canada (especially Québec) and the United States. The construction of new monasteries, convents, schools and hospitals

175 Film *Of Gods and Men*, by Xavier Beauvois, 2010 [original title: *Des Hommes et des Dieux*].

176 In England 825 monasteries were dissolved and demolished by order of the king in the years 1536-41. Woodward, *The Dissolution of the Monasteries*. About France: Réau, *Histoire du vandalisme*.

177 Cabanel and Durand, *Le grand exil des congrégations religieuses françaises*.

accompanied these transfers. This explains in particular why Belgium and Québec have a monastic heritage that is not in keeping with the size of their population, but also why the problem of the reuse of religious houses is so significant in these two countries.

In a way, the abandonment, transfer and destruction of religious establishments are inseparable from the very activity of foundation; they are part of the monastic history and identity of religious congregations. This may seem paradoxical in view of the stability, eternal dimensional and symbolism of the Heavenly Jerusalem present in monastic foundations [see Chapters 5 and 15]. Yet, from the spiritual perspective of the monks and nuns, the dimension of eternity is on a different level from that of laymen, and they will see a transfer merely as an accident of history, or even a trial set by God. For the monk, in fact, the sacred is much less present in architecture than in the divine office, the liturgy, prayer, hospitality and the relationship with one's neighbour.[178]

The Christian world is therefore littered with ruins of religious houses: monasteries of the Desert Fathers in Egypt, early Christian abbeys in Syria, abbeys and commandries in the Holy Land, Irish Celtic monasteries [Fig. 7], abbeys and priories in England [Fig. 23, 53 and 64], Jesuit *reductiones* in Brazil and Paraguay, ruins left strewn across Europe by the French Revolution [Fig. 18], etc. Abandoned, sometimes even forgotten, these ruins have served as quarries for materials. Everything with a market value was sold and they ultimately survived as mere carcasses which, in turn, were subject to the erosion of time. Several centuries later, hundreds of sites of ruined abbeys have been heritagised and turned into tourist attractions, in the same way as ruins of Greek or Roman antiquity. They are shown off to their best advantage and have often found a new balance in the landscape. How was this point reached?

The awareness of an interest in ruined abbeys, firstly by Romantic poets and painters in search of ghosts and other picturesque sensations, then by historians and archaeologists from a nationalistic perspective, came into being in England in the mid-eighteenth century and spread across Europe in the wake of revolutionary vandalism. From the early nineteenth century, the ruins of the medieval Christian West aroused as much curiosity as those of ancient civilisations.[179] They attracted artists, historians, archaeologists and tourists and gradually became heritage sites. [Fig. 87]

Stages of heritagisation varied from one site to another, but in general the following questions were asked at some point in the process: are they privately or publicly owned?; should the State expropriate a private property in the name of public interest?; what sort of tourist development should be considered?; how should the ruin be restored or maintained?; why or how

178 Veilleux, 'What makes a Monastery a Sacred Place?'.

179 For example: Taylor, Nodier and de Cailleux, *Voyages pittoresques et romantiques dans l'ancienne France.*

Fig. 87. Ruins of the Cistercian abbey of Melrose (Scotland), source of inspiration for Walter Scott and many other romantic artists.
[© THOC]

should archaeological excavations be organised? [Fig. 11, 65 and 71]; should the return of religious communities be stimulated?; are there any other suitable uses?; what cultural activity developments or multimedia showcasing should be considered? The successive stages of heritagisation of a large complex of medieval monastic ruins are well illustrated by the case of the former Cistercian abbey of Villers, the perception of which evolved, over two centuries, from Romanticism to New Age.[180] [Fig. 18]

Ruin was not necessarily accompanied by the abandonment of the monastic site and may have only been a temporary state linked to an avatar of history as a fact of war. The example *par excellence* is the Abbey of Monte Cassino, birthplace of Benedictine monasticism in circa 530, where Saint Benedict composed the Rule and was buried. The abbey found itself at the centre of the Battle of Montecassino, which was the fiercest of the Italian Campaign (February-July 1944). Completely ruined, it was rebuilt in its pre-war state by the Italian government. Such a reconstruction aims to erase the accident of history and not to interrupt the long period of monastic history and tradition. [Fig. 51]

180 Coomans, 'Heritagization of an Abbey Ruin'; Id., *L'abbaye de Villers-en-Brabant*, 19-32.

22. Manors, Farms and Factories

In the sixteenth century, following the redistribution of abbey property by the King of England to his most loyal courtiers, many abbeys were converted into manor houses or country residences.[181] These developed in one or other of the abbey's buildings, sometimes in a part of the church (Titchfield Abbey) or a wing of the cloister (Hailes Abbey) [Fig. 88], sometimes in a peripheral building such as the gatehouse (Beaulieu Abbey), guesthouse (Fountains Abbey) or the former abbot's lodgings (Forde Abbey). Ruined, the other buildings disappeared over time, or became focal points for English landscape gardens (Gisborough Priory, Fountains Abbey at Studley Royal) or grandiose elements of the landscape (Glastonbury Abbey, Lindisfarne Abbey, Whitby Abbey). [Fig. 53] A similar phenomenon took place in the German principalities that had become Protestant. In 1552, the Cistercian abbey of Dargun became a hunting residence (*Jagdschloss*) of the dukes of Mecklenburg-Güstrow, who kept the church and converted the three wings around the former cloister into an elegant Renaissance residence.[182] Schloss Mildenfurth is a Renaissance château with an unusual cruciform plan: it was in fact the church of a thirteenth-century Premonstratensian abbey. An advisor to the Duke of Thuringia demolished most of the monastic buildings and transformed parts of the nave, transepts and choir of the church into a château.[183] The large castle and its crossing tower dominate the surroundings as the abbey had done for several centuries earlier. [Fig. 89]

In England, the 'Gothic abbey' eventually became a new type of château. The most famous château imitating an abbey was Fonthill Abbey, built by the eccentric William Thomas Beckford from 1795 to 1813, a time when abbeys were being destroyed in their hundreds across France.[184]

The suppression of abbeys in France in the late eighteenth century led to the destruction of churches and monastic buildings because they were no longer of any use. Abbey farms and mills merely changed ownership and retained their function. As in England in the sixteenth century, the lodgings of many abbots and abbesses became mansions with grounds. This explains why some monastic sites retain only their farm and abbot's or abbess' residence, and why the site of the church, cloister and monastic buildings form a gap between the residence, now a château, and the farm.[185] Many churches and cloisters were destroyed or simply collapsed through lack of maintenance. They

181 Coppack, *Abbeys and Priories*, 12-20.
182 Kratzke, *Das Zisterzienserkloster Dargun*.
183 Eichhorn, 'Der einstige Prämonstratenserkloster und Schlosskomplex Mildenfurth'.
184 Unfortunately demolished before the mid-nineteenth century: Wilton-Ely, 'The Genesis and Evolution of Fonthill Abbey'.
185 For example at the female abbeys of Herkenrode and La Ramée: Coomans, *La Ramée*, 133-196.

Fig. 88. Remains of the Cistercian abbey of Hailes (England) converted into a manor house next to the ruined cloister, engraving by Samuel Buck, 1732.
[http://edkluz.tumblr.com]

had lost their use value. Elsewhere, fragments of churches remained ruined alongside a château built in a wing of monastic buildings, as in the former abbeys of Longpont, Vaux-de-Cernay, Ourscamp and Chaalis near Paris. In the middle of a romantic park, the Abbey of Loc-Dieu was converted between 1884-87 into a medieval château with towers and crenellations.

Some churches escaped the destruction by receiving an agricultural function: a grange or even a large cellar or wine storehouse, such as the abbey church of Valmagne. More simply, many abbey churches were converted into granges or farm sheds [Fig. 90], while the chapter house and other vaulted rooms around the cloister became stables and manure occupied the centre of the former cloister's courtyard. Such was the lot of many small rural monasteries in France, whose heritagisation and enhancement did not really begin until after the Second World War, or even more recently, following the difficulties encountered by farmers confronted with European agricultural reforms. It was by seeking a new use for these abbeys-turned-farms and former monastic granges that their heritage value was discovered, resulting in them being taken over by the local community in order to protect the sites.[186]

With the birth of the industrial age, many monasteries located in valleys were converted into factories and played a part in the industrial revolution at the start of the nineteenth century. The proximity of watercourses favoured such conversions because water could drive mills and trip hammers in forges, as well as power steam engines. Saint Benedict, who had wished for the

186 Pressouyre, *L'espace cistercien.*

Fig. 89. Former church of the Premonstratensian abbey of Mildenfurth (Germany), converted into a château in the sixteenth century and recent urbanisation of the site.
[© Dr. Jürgen Zehe]

presence of water and mills inside monastic enclosures [see Chapter 2], had obviously not foreseen these industrial developments. Abbey churches were transformed into factories: a glassworks at Val-Saint-Lambert [Fig. 91], cotton spinning at the Abbey of Auberive, forges at the Abbey of Moulins, a sugar beet factory at La Ramée, etc. It is hard to imagine that the Abbey of Fontenay, one of the monastic gems of World Heritage, was home to a paper mill from 1820 to 1903.[187] Old photographs show the site during the industrial age in which the church is flanked by tall factory chimneys.

In Ghent, one of the first towns on the European continent to develop industrial textile production, the Carmelite friary became a spinning mill and its church was split into several storeys to maximise usable surface area. The same industrialist converted the former Premonstratensian abbey in Drongen into a spinning mill: a steam engine took centre stage in the middle of the cloister and used belts to power dozens of spinning mules set up throughout the monastic buildings.[188] The order of the cloister suited the rational layout of the factory but the noise and vibrations of the machine drowned out the silence of the enclosed garden.

187 André, 'La papeterie des Mongolfier à Fontenay'.
188 Decavele et al., eds, *De Oude Abdij van Drongen*, 289-301.

Fig. 90. Former Cistercian nunnery of Argenton (Belgium), converted into a farm from 1796: the abbesses' residence became the farmhouse and the chapel a barn; the other monastic buildings disappeared. [© THOC]

23. Residential Use

Another way of making urban converts immediately profitable after their suppression was to convert them into residential buildings. This was not as relevant to their churches but to the buildings around the cloister, and responded to the housing crisis in the emerging industrial cities of the early nineteenth century. These were not luxury homes but slums, the exploitation of which benefited unscrupulous slum landlords. With its inward-looking morphology inside a block, urban religious houses lent themselves to this type of speculation, with cloisters serving as internal courtyards and the large rooms subdivided to maximise yield. In most cases, such reuse was not sustainable over the long term and further speculation gradually replaced the old buildings with new and more profitable real estate projects.

The reuse of abbeys, monasteries and convents as hotels is a more recent phenomenon that has acquired a new dimension in recent decades. Examples of good and less good taste proliferate. Could this be tourism's way of searching for authenticity or even silence? Or simply a rejection of the bland products of big hotel chains in favour of personalised formulas and a 'historical experience'? This movement originated in Spain, where, from 1928, the government

Fig. 91. On the site of the former Cistercian abbey of Val-Saint-Lambert in Seraing (Belgium) developed from 1826 the glassworks factory Cristalleries du Val-Saint-Lambert, now a post-industrial site. [© SPAQuE, Liège]

transformed châteaux and abbeys into luxury hotels called '*paradores*'.[189] Portugal followed suit in 1941 with its chain of '*pousadas*', which also includes several monasteries. [Fig. 84] In France, the '*Hôtels France Patrimoine*' network opened a hotel in the heart of the Abbey of Fontevraud, a UNESCO World Heritage site, in March 2010.[190] These networks are part of the Historic Hotels of Europe platform, which includes an increasing number of abbeys as well as châteaux.[191] The formula that combines heritage, gastronomy and design seems to be a winning one, and the experience of spending a few days of rest and luxury inside a historical cloister, in a secluded spot or town, has clearly found a certain audience.[192] 'Life in a cell can be heaven (when it's an ex-convent)' can be read on the promotional website for one of these monasteries-turned-hotels.[193]

189 There are currently 92 *paradores* in Spain, including 14 that occupy former monasteries: <http://www.paradores-spain.com/>.
190 Also, the abbeys of Saint-Maximin and Sorèze, <http://www.hotels-francepatrimoine.com/groupe/>.
191 <http://www.historichotelsofeurope.com>.
192 For example: San Clemente Palace Kempinski in Venice; Monastero Santa Rosa near Conca dei Marini; Couvent des Minimes Hôtel & Spa in Mane near Manosque.
193 <https://www.pousadas.pt/en/hotel/pousada-evora/reviews> (accessed October 2017).

In Rome, most international religious orders have a house or motherhouse, and sometimes also seminaries or training centres. The crisis in vocations and maintenance costs of these buildings have inspired more than one order to convert them into guesthouses to accommodate pilgrims and tourists. In other places of pilgrimage or major tourist cities, such as Venice, religious institutes have converted their monasteries into reception centres or hotels, often equipped with facilities for meetings or seminars.

Many monasteries and convents have been converted into nursing and retirement homes. These are not generally historical monuments, but nineteenth- and twentieth-century complexes that could easily be brought up to standard. The cloister forms an internal garden, the calm of which is much appreciated. The origin of such reuse dates back to the French Revolution, when the care of those disinherited by private religious charitable institutions was replaced by the 'charity offices' (*bureaux de bienfaisance*). Public welfare services often began operating in former monasteries that were available because they had recently been secularised. Furthermore, in the present context of ageing communities, some religious houses are being converted into houses for elderly monks and nuns.

24. Barracks, Arsenals, Prisons and Courthouses

The requisitioning of monasteries for the purposes of barracking troops has always taken place during times of war. The rational organisation of buildings around a cloister and courtyards, as well as the presence of large rooms (church, refectory, dormitories, etc.) and logistical infrastructure (fountain, sanitary facilities, kitchen, farm, mill), provided effective collective housing for a regiment in the field, an urban garrison, a military hospital or even a supply depot. Once the war had finished and the troops had departed, the religious communities recovered the buildings and re-consecrated the church if it had been profaned, so that everything could 'return to order'.

During the sixteenth-century wars of religion and the French Revolution, in the context of the establishment of military states, the need for barracks, arsenals and prisons found an adequate solution in suppressed monasteries. Friaries located near city gates and walls were particularly favourable. An ordered and self-contained architecture suited the maintenance of troop discipline. Usually emptied of their contents, these buildings were laid out according to their new programme, which required maximum square footage. Churches were often subdivided into several levels using wooden floors. The former Franciscan friary in Maastricht and its late thirteenth-century Gothic church became an arsenal in 1639 after the Protestants took the town.[194]

194 Dingemans, *De oude Minderbroeders*; Spijkerman, *Het Rijksarchief Limburg*.

Fig. 92. Nave of the former Franciscan church in Maastricht (The Netherlands), late thirteenth century, used as an arsenal, engraving from 1759.
[© Regionaal Historisch Centrum Limburg, Maastricht]

Divided into several storeys, the former church was considered a model arsenal to the extent that a series of engravings demonstrating the interior layout was published in 1759. This series of plans, sections and perspectives forms an extremely valuable iconographic source and illustrates a common practice. [Fig. 92]

In Antwerp, the great Premonstratensian abbey of Saint Michael's was secularised in 1796 and used as an arsenal. Located along the river Scheldt it soon became a marine arsenal and wharf where the French fleet for the invasion of England was built.[195] Napoleon himself examined the plans for this strategic investment. Because of their rational layout, only the main wings around the cloister and the abbey church survived, the latter being divided into four floors. New buildings such as a forge were built on the site and a semaphore was installed on top of the tower. [Fig. 93] Under subsequent Dutch rule, the arsenal became a barracks, which burned down during the Belgian Revolution in 1830. Thereafter, the site was cleared and new houses were built along new streets.

Over time, the majority of these military establishments lost their function and the army built new, rational barracks on more appropriate sites. Many of these former monastic buildings were destroyed because they were in poor condition, their location was favourable to urban development and their heritage value had yet to be recognised.

195 Klaarenbeek and Coomans, 'From Guessing to 'Gissing''.

Fig. 93. Former Premonstratensian abbey of Saint Michael in Antwerp, used as a marine arsenal, shipyard and semaphore, 1804-15.
[© Royal Library of Belgium, Prints Department, Brussels]

In the early days of the French Revolution, prisons were improvised in monasteries. The Carmes friary in Paris served as a prison and was the scene of religious massacres in September 1792. Louis XVI and Marie-Antoinette were imprisoned in the Tower of the Temple, which had become a state prison after the suppression of the Knights Templars in 1312. After the Terror in 1794, a new prison model based on criminal detention was introduced. Prisons became places for the deprivation of liberty and transformation of the individual. As in the monastic model, isolation and solitude were, according to Michel Foucault, not only conducive to order and control but also to reflection: 'the cell places the detainee in the presence of himself; he is forced to listen to his conscience'.[196] From the 1830s onwards, architectural programmes developed that were specific to prisons and the building of 'prison machines' began. As a result, the enclosed courtyard no longer provided the model for panopticon or the star-shaped prisons. However, the abbeys of Mont-Saint-Michel and Fontevraud, two icons of medieval monastic architecture, served as prisons from 1793 to 1863 and from 1804 to 1963 respectively. This use guaranteed the maintenance of buildings at a time when barely any thought was given to heritage. Their subsequent heritagisation gradually led to their protection, restoration, conversion and finally their inclusion on the World Heritage list in 1979 and 2000. [Fig. 103] Despite being classified as a historic monument in 1926, Clairvaux, the abbey of Saint Bernard, still serves as a prison.[197]

196 Foucault, *Surveiller et punir*, 241.
197 Leroux, 'La prison'.

Fig. 94. Former Franciscan friary in Maastricht (The Netherlands) converted into a 'Maison d'arrêt', picture from 1915.
[© Regionaal Historisch Centrum Limburg, Maastricht]

The 'maison d'arrêt' is a specific category of prison where people are held as they await their judgement and sentencing, or are condemned to short term imprisonment. These prisons are ideally located near the courthouse in order to avoid long transfers. After the French Revolution and the reorganisation of the justice, many churches were converted into courthouses, while the cloister and adjacent buildings served as jails. Several, such as the former Carmelite convent in Chartres, are still in use today.

After been expelled from Maastricht in 1639 and losing their medieval monastery that became an arsenal [Fig. 92], the Franciscans returned to Maastricht in 1699 and built a second monastery in the town. The latter was secularised in 1796 by the French, who converted the church into a courthouse and the neighbouring buildings into a jail. Old plans and photographs show how the church and the rooms around the cloister were subdivided for their new use. [Fig. 95] The church windows were all adapted to the new floor levels and those of the cells reduced to small openings. [Fig. 94] The court and prison moved to another site in 1995 and the buildings were eventually converted into the rector's office and central administration of Maastricht University.

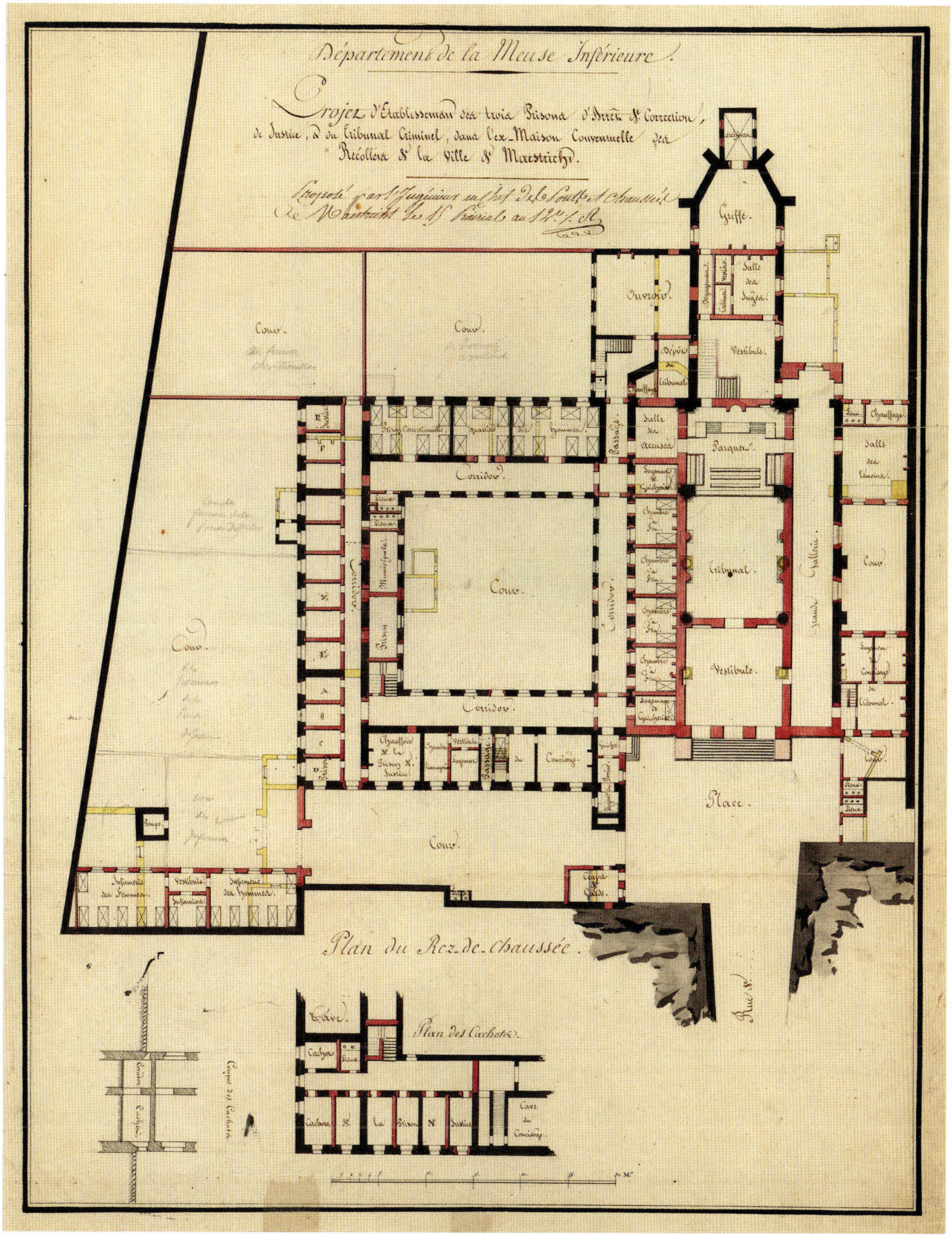

Fig. 95. Former Franciscan friary in Maastricht (The Netherlands) converted into a 'Maison d'arrêt': the church served as court and the convent's buildings as a prison; plan from 1804.
[© Regionaal Historisch Centrum Limburg, Maastricht]

25. University Colleges and Lyceums

In the sixteenth century, during the Reformation, the new Protestant rulers founded universities in suppressed monasteries so that they would become educational centres for the newly reformed elite. Thus the Dominican friaries of Leipzig and Groningen became the starting points for new universities. The first buildings of the University of Leiden, founded in 1575, were the chapels of suppressed convents. That of the Dominican nunnery split into three levels for classrooms. Known as the *Academiegebouw* (academic building), it is still used today for academic sessions, notably the defence of doctorates. The church of Leiden's beguinage was also divided into several storeys and served for a long time as an anatomical amphitheatre and university library before becoming the seat of the rectorate.[198] In 1543, the Duke of Saxony opened an elite school in the former Cistercian abbey of Pforta (Schulpforta) that had just been suppressed; it became one of the best in the country and was attended by the mathematician Möbius and the philosophers Fichte and Nietzsche.

The architectural type of the medieval university college with cloister galleries, a chapel and a large refectory has a shared origin with the mendicant friary and dates back to the thirteenth century. Mendicant orders founded friaries specialising in theological studies at universities (*studium*). The majority of lay colleges, the Sorbonne in Paris foremost among them, copied the morphology of mendicant *studia* because it favoured the discipline and order indispensable to successful learning.[199] When Henry VIII abolished religious orders in England some friaries in university towns served as starting points for new colleges, including Christ Church College, Trinity College and St John's College in Oxford and Emmanuel College and Jesus College in Cambridge. Beyond these few historical cases, the architectural type of the university college in the English Gothic style, like those of Cambridge and Oxford, became the model for university colleges and elite schools in the Anglo-Saxon world in the nineteenth century, right up until the 1950s in the United States.

During the French Revolution, many urban religious houses were converted into lay schools, secondary schools, military schools and fine arts academies. Several have often remained so to the present day.[200] The Republic introduced a new education policy that required buildings that promoted order and discipline. Thanks to their regular morphology and enclosure, friaries lent themselves particularly well to this conversion. Among numerous examples in France, the most famous are the Lycée Henri IV in the former Abbey of Sainte-Geneviève in Paris and the Prytanée National Militaire in the former Jesuit Collège Royal Henri-Le-Grand at La Flèche. [Fig. 41] In Belgium, the former Benedictine abbey of Gembloux became an agricultural school in

198 *Universiteit & Architectuur. Ontwerpen voor de Leidse Universiteit.*
199 Rückbrod, *Universität und Kollegium*, 38-62.
200 Klaarenbeek and Coomans, 'Reusing Urban Convents as State Schools'.

Fig. 96. Former Benedictine abbey of Sant' Ambrogio in Milan (Italy), cloister designed by Bramante in 1497-98, seat of the Università Cattolica del Sacro Cuore from 1921.
[© THOC]

1860 and is now the Faculty of Agronomic Sciences at the University of Liège. [Fig. 45] In Milan, the Università Cattolica del Sacro Cuore was founded in 1921 in the former Benedictine abbey of Sant' Ambrogio and enjoys the great Renaissance cloister designed by Bramante in 1497-98. [Fig. 95] In many schools, chapels have been converted into sport halls.

The adaptive reuse of monasteries, friaries and convents as university buildings remains current. Growing universities are looking for urban properties for academic use or student housing. Large nineteenth-century religious houses, often with listed buildings and gardens, are thus able to benefit from public subsidies and contribute to the prestige of the universities. The case of the motherhouse of the Sisters of Charity (Grey Sisters) in Montreal, acquired by Concordia University in 2007, is a good illustration of this phenomenon.[201] In the centre of Bruges, the College of Europe bought the buildings of the former Jesuit college in 1995, which had been suppressed in 1773 and used subsequently as an *athenaeum* and state school. In 2007, the College of Europe opened an urban campus on a site that harmoniously juxtaposes new educational buildings with those that date from the seventeenth century.

Often, the cloisters of small urban religious houses have been covered and are used as central halls. The former convent of the Grey Sisters in Antwerp, converted into the rectorate of the University of Antwerp in 2006, is a

201 Noppen and Morisset, 'La renaissance des couvents au Québec', 124.

Fig. 97. Former convent of the Grey Sisters in Antwerp (Belgium), now the rectorate of the University of Antwerp, by VBM architecten, 2006.
[© Oswald Pauwels / Agentschap Onroerend Erfgoed]

typical example of such adaptive reuse: the cloister became a hall covered with a glass structure and an underground auditorium has been built underneath. [Fig. 97]

Since the 1960s, the University of Leuven has regularly acquired former religious properties, either those built in the nineteenth and twentieth centuries or older buildings that were occupied by religious communities until recently. The jewel in the crown of its heritage is the beguinage, included on the UNESCO World Heritage list in 1998, whose some hundred houses serve as accommodation for foreign students, while the church is used as the university parish.[202] [Fig. 33] Reuses are varied and include among others: the Faculty of Theology (former Jesuit residence and college), the campus Library of Sciences and Technology (former Celestine Priory) [Fig. 98], KADOC, Documentation and Research Center on Religion, Culture and Society (former Franciscan friary), a hospital for children (late medieval charterhouse, turned into a convent of Capuchins in the nineteenth century), Metaforum, Centre for Societal Debate (Dutch College, later nunnery), the Faculty of Architecture (former Dominican friary in Ghent), student housing (former convent of the Black Sisters, and former American College), university administration (nineteenth-

202 Uytterhoeven, *The Groot Begijnhof of Leuven*.

Fig. 98. Former Celestine Priory in Leuven (Belgium), converted into the Library of Sciences and Technology at the University of Leuven by architect Rafael Moneo in 1996-2002.
[© THOC]

century residence of the Jesuits), etc. This variety of adaptive reuses illustrates the high potential of former urban monasteries, according to their diversity of building types, size, original use, style, gender, etc.

26. The Sacredness of Culture

After the French Revolution, the secular republican society introduced new public institutions aimed at ensuring and developing a new worldview. Buildings were therefore required to house these new institutions of public education, justice, hospitals and museums. Therefore, many recently suppressed urban religious houses looking for a new use became schools, courthouses, hospitals, libraries, theatres and museums. They were also part of the new 'sacred mission' of republican values – liberty, equality, fraternity –, especially for the education of future generations and the development of culture. The peace of former cloisters would contribute to promote new meditation.

In the typology of new uses for monastic buildings, museums occupy a special place. The most emblematic example of such a shift in meaning was the famous *Musée des Monuments français* in Paris, founded in 1791 by

Alexandre Lenoir in the former friary of the Petits-Augustins to save the masterpieces of sculpture from destruction.[203] It was precisely at the moment when revolutionary vandalism destroyed a huge number of works of the past that a heritage awareness came into being. Due to their availability on the real estate market and architectural qualities, some urban religious houses became the earliest public museums in France, established in August 1801 by the 'Arrêté Chaptal'. Several of these museum still exist today, such as the *Musée des Arts et Métiers* in Paris, in the former priory of Saint-Martin-des-Champs, the *Musée des Beaux-Arts* in Toulouse, in the former Augustinian friary, and the *Musée des Beaux-Arts* in Lyon, in the former royal abbey of the Dames de Saint-Pierre.

In modern-day France, large abbeys secularised and heritagised as national monuments are often managed by public authorities, who are able to develop high-level cultural programmes with generous budgets. For example, the *Maison des écrivains et de la littérature* occupies the monastery of Saorge; the *Institut mémoires de l'édition contemporaine* occupies the Abbey of Ardenne near Caen; and the *Centre national des écritures du spectacle* occupies the Charterhouse of Villeneuve-lès-Avignon, etc.[204] In the latter, the writers in residence each stay in a Carthusian cell around the cloister. In addition to the large state-owned monuments, run by the Centre for National Monuments, such as the abbeys of Mont-Saint-Michel, Fontevraud, Cluny, Le Thoronet, Montmajour, etc., other abbeys are managed by local authorities that join forces to create centres of cultural action such as the Abbey of Saint-Savin-sur-Gartempe. About the half of the forty monuments that constitute the network of the Association of Cultural Encounter Centres are former abbeys or monasteries.[205]

The number of abbeys, monasteries and convents around the world that are being reused as museums is significant, so much so that the cloister, patio or internal garden with fountain have become popular components of the museum typology. Countless former abbeys, monasteries and convents across Europe and Latin America have become museums of religious art, sacred art, medieval art and ancient art. This choice is based on a desire to preserve the spirit of the place [see Conclusion]. The following are just a handful of examples: the Museum Catharijneconvent in Utrecht, the Museum Schnütgen in the former nunnery of Saint Cecilia in Cologne, the Diocesan museum of Milan in the cloister of Sant'Eustorgio, Parcum – the Museum for religion, art and culture in the Norbertine abbey of Park near Leuven [Fig. 72], the National Gallery of Art in the convent of Saint Agnes of Bohemia in Prague, the Musée Unterlinden in the former Dominican convent in Colmar, the Museo Nazionale di San Marco in Florence and the Hôpital Notre-Dame à la Rose in Lessines.

203 Poulot, 'Alexandre Lenoir'.

204 Chevrefils Desbiolles, *L'Abbaye d'Ardenne*; Sournia and Vayssettes, *Villeneuve-lès-Avignon*; <http://www.chartreuse.org>.

205 This European network gathers professionals exploring the interaction between heritage, research and contemporary creation, <https://www.accr-europe.org>.

Fig. 99. Romanesque cloister of the Benedictine abbey of Saint-Michel-de-Cuxa (France), disassembled and shipped to New York, now part of the Cloisters Museum.
[© THOC]

Conversely, the medieval art museum The Cloisters in New York, built in 1935-38, consists of five Romanesque cloisters bought in France, transplanted and reassembled into a museum along Hudson River.[206] This museum is therefore a fictive abbey composed of fragments of real abbeys. [Fig. 99]

Contemporary art museums are in search of large, bright spaces and prefer therefore to build new architecture rather than to make do with former monasteries. However, several examples show that contemporary art can work well with the austerity of old cloisters: the Centro Andaluz de Arte Contemporáneo in the Charterhouse of Santa María de Las Cuevas in Seville [Fig. 100], the Kunstmuseum Kloster Unser Lieben Frauen in Magdeburg in a Premonstratensian abbey, the National Museum of Contemporary Art in the former São Francisco da Cidade friary in Lisbon, the Museum of Photography in Charleroi in a former Carmelite convent, etc. Elsewhere, parts of monasteries are integrated into larger museum complexes such as the former charterhouse of Nuremberg in the Germanisches Nationalmuseum or the former Cistercian abbey and hospital complex of Byloke in the STAM-City Museum of Ghent. Sometimes, the theme of the Museum is incongruous, such as the Spa-Francorchamps Circuit Museum in the former Abbey of Stavelot. [Fig. 11] Reuse is a never-ending process in an evolving society that does not hide its post-modern taste for the eclectic and unusual.

206 Barnet and Wu, *The Cloisters*, 9-19.

Fig. 100. Former Charterhouse of Seville (Spain), turned into a pottery factory in the mid-nineteenth century, in 1992 into the Centro Andaluz de Arte Contemporaneo.
[© Arco Images GmbH / Alamy Stock Photo]

The conversion of monasteries and convents into cultural centres and their churches into theatres or libraries is also common. The monastic tradition has always placed great emphasis on writing and study. Medieval monks wrote, copied, illuminated and bound manuscript books, and some communities began printing books before the end of the fifteenth century. Books were present in every abbey, ranging from a few obligatory basic texts for the divine office and meditation (Bible, psalter, evangelary, antiphonary, lectionary, obituary, etc.) to large libraries that could hold several tens of thousands of books on a variety of subjects (theology, philosophy, hagiography, history, natural sciences, literature, etc.), not to mention archives produced over centuries of existence (charters, cartularies, accounts, land ownership atlases, etc.). The male monasteries, friaries and houses of 'intellectual' orders –Benedictines, Jesuits, Cistercians, Premonstratensians, Carthusians, Dominicans, Carmelites, Franciscans and the other mendicant orders – developed large libraries in particular in their study centres linked to universities. [Fig. 76] Today, the late Baroque library of the Benedictine abbey of Admont in Austria is considered the largest monastic library in the world[207] but many others were demolished or dispersed during the French Revolution. [Fig. 104]

Libraries and archives are therefore inseparable from the monastic identity, and the reuse of a monastery as a library or archive centre has a particu-

207 With more than 200,000 printed books, 1400 manuscripts and 530 incunabula <https://www.stiftadmont.at/>.

Fig. 101. The former Franciscan friary in Maastricht (Netherlands), converted into the regional historical centre of the Province of Limburg; the church serves as a reading room.
[© THOC]

lar cultural significance. The earliest reuses date back to the aftermath of the French Revolution, when the archives and libraries of suppressed religious houses were gathered up by the State and showcased in public institutions. The municipal library of Saint-Omer, housed in the former Jesuit residence and college, and Zurich's Zentralbibliothek in the former Dominican friary are just some examples. A problem inherent to archives and libraries is the growth of their collections and the optimisation of conservation conditions. When a building or site is listed, it is not always possible to extend it and ingenious solutions are sometimes implemented, including the development of large underground reserves beneath the cloister or garden. Such is the case of the Franciscan friary in Maastricht, which, after serving as an arsenal, became the Province of Limburg Archives [Figs 92 and 101], or the KADOC in Leuven, another former Franciscan friary converted into an archive for religious institutes in Flanders,[208] or the university science library in Leuven in a former Celestine Priory converted by the architect Rafael Moneo in 1996-2002.[209] [Fig. 98]

In 2006, the Gothic Dominican church in Maastricht, after years of abandonment and uncertainty, was converted masterfully by Merkx+Girod into a bookshop (Selexyz Dominicanen) by building several storeys of shelving on top of a lateral metal structure. The same is true of the former Dominican church in Zwolle (Waanders In de Broeren), converted in 2013. We could say that cultural consumers are a new kind of churchgoers.

208 De Maeyer and Suenens, 'Le patrimoine historique et culturel des instituts religieux'.
209 Derez and Verbrugge, *The Celestine Priory at Leuven*.

Fig. 102. Cloister of the convent of the Canonesses Regular of the Holy Sepulchre established in 1974 on the site of the former medieval Cistercian nunnery of Herkenrode (Belgium).
[© THOC]

CONCLUSION

TRADITION, HERITAGE AND THE SPIRIT OF THE PLACE

With a multiple, dense and rich heritage, monastic architecture is not easy to understand in its nuances, specific features and complexity. In the first three sections of this book on 'Life inside the Cloister', we provided keys to gaining access to this complexity. However, a fourth section focusing on the afterlife of monastic architecture has also been necessary as the present situation in the monastic world is unprecedented. Due to a lack of reform and succession, the Western monastic world is currently experiencing a profound crisis. The challenge now seems to be one of tangible, intangible and even spiritual monastic memory. Of what, why, to whom and how to pass this on. The magnitude of heritage awareness we are witnessing reveals the gravity of the situation, as work to remember begins precisely at the moment when meaning is lost.

This book has often made mention of tradition (*tradere*, to transmit), the monastic tradition in particular, or rather the handing down from generation to generation of the essence of monasticism itself, or other forms of religious community life.[210] Each monastic order and religious family has its own tradition based on its rule, constitutions and other founding spiritual texts that define the spiritual, legal and liturgical aspects of the life of these communities. Religious traditions are inscribed in places and also include the memory of people, both holy people and otherwise. Therefore the Benedictine tradition

210 With the apostolic tradition – which goes back to Christ through the intermediary of his first disciples –, all monastic traditions are part of the Christian tradition that is based on the New Testament.

differs strongly from the Jesuit tradition, and so on. The challenge of communities is to keep their tradition alive while adapting to the reality of society and the Church. By doing so they continue this tradition and ensure that it will be passed on.

This book has also often mentioned the issue of heritage (*heritare*, to receive from a succession), something one inherits and passes on, rather than patrimony (*patrimonium*, a father's goods or fortune), something one receives and is responsible for developing.[211] In this discussion of monastic architecture, heritage means the transmitted cultural goods in their immovable and tangible forms, as well as their interaction with movable tangible goods and intangible forms. Without being synonyms, the concepts of tradition and heritage share some common ground. It is clear that monastic cultural heritage is part of the monastic tradition or at least the expression of it. It can also be said that Christian monastic tradition is part of the legacy of Christianity but also of Western civilisation and heritage.

The link between religious tradition and monastic architecture is undoubtedly the 'spirit of the place', which, to return to the formula, is 'between tangible and intangible heritage'.[212] Pierre Lucier's reflections on spiritual traditions and the spirit of the place perfectly express the key point of the conclusion to this book:

> Between the spirituality of religious families, the architectural design of their religious houses and buildings and the means of their presence and action, there are correspondences that count for much in the *spirit of the place* contained in these complexes. It is this *spirit of the place* that constitutes the foundation of the cultural significance of religious houses that, if their authentic heritage value is recognised, can provide guidelines for profane reuse likely to respect and prolong their symbolic potential.[213]

The closure of a monastery or a convent is usually accompanied by a break in the tradition of the religious family but not in its heritage. When a monastery is closed and its church deconsecrated, 'the key question is whether this gesture is enough to efface the complexity of the meanings embodied in a [monastery] at different scales and levels, transforming it into a simple container in which new use can be installed'.[214] At this very precise moment the specific challenge facing religious heritage arises: how can the shift from the sacredness of religion to the sacredness of heritage and culture be made

211 Morisset, 'Patrimony, the Concept', 54-56.

212 Turgeon, *Spirit of Place: Between Tangible and Intangible Heritage*; Id., *Le patrimoine religieux du Québec: entre le culturel et le cultuel.*

213 Lucier, 'Traditions spirituelles et esprit du lieu', 481.

214 Albani, 'New Lives for Deconsacrated Churches', 11.

Fig. 103. Benedictine abbey of Mont-Saint-Michel (France), cloister, 1225-28.
[© Jose Ignacio Soto/123RF Stock Photo]

successfully? Is such a transfer possible without a loss of meaning, without losing the *spirit of the place*? It is here that education in religious heritage intervenes, with its secular, religious, tangible and intangible concerns.[215]

What should the response be to a genuine demand from 'heritage tourist/pilgrims' or 'religious pilgrim/tourists'? Monastic sites, whether living or secularised, religious or profane, ruined or filled with art treasures, continue to attract a great many visitors whose motivations are varied. Many are in search of points of reference, silence, a slower pace or even spirituality in one form or another. These needs seem to belong to a society 'exculturated of Catholicism' and have been analysed by sociologists.[216]

We have seen that many reuses carried out without a concern for heritage or architectural and archaeological knowledge have more often than not led to a trivialisation and loss of meaning [see Chapters 21 to 24]. However, through appropriate heritage restoration, architectural complexes debased in this way have succeeded in rediscovering the spirit of the place without the need to re-establish a monastic community or re-consecrate the church. One thinks of the Abbey of Fontenay, secularised, privatised and turned into a paper mill, which, thanks to the efforts of experts (including Viollet-le-Duc),

215 Lefebvre, *Le patrimoine religieux du Québec. Éducation et transmission du sens.*
216 Voyé, 'The Need and the Search for Sacred Places'.

private owners, and restoration architects, became a national monument and was eventually included on the UNESCO World Heritage list, in accordance with criterion (iv), in 1981.[217] In museums, libraries and other cultural buildings, monastic cloister galleries and gardens find another sacred dimension [see Chapters 25 and 26]. Plenty of other reuses are possible if heritage awareness and knowledge of the specific tradition of the place, its spirit, are combined. The concern for authenticity remains an essential condition to the safeguarding of the spirit of the place: seeing pretend monks promote so-called monastic products or real monks selling more or less traditional products only generates ambiguities and misunderstandings.[218]

In one way or another, and to varying degrees, all monastic architectural complexes are palimpsests [see Chapter 19], some of which exhibit incredible overlappings of style and use, even including new religious practices after a phase of secularisation. Two examples among many others – one rural, the other urban – illustrate that monastic architectural history is generally much more turbulent than one might imagine.

In Drongen, near Ghent, a secular chapter (tenth century) was reformed and became a Premonstratensian abbey (1138), then ruined and abandoned during the religious wars (1566-1609), rebuilt during the Counter-Reformation (seventeenth century), suppressed during the French Revolution (1797), then sold and converted into an industrial spinning mill and dye factory. Bought in two phases by the Jesuits (1837-48), they turned it into their provincial training centre and a retreat centre for the laity (until 1968). The buildings and the site are listed (1998) and became, after the departure of the Jesuits, an 'Ignatian centre for Christian spirituality'.[219]

The Franciscan friary of the Recollects in Paris, built from 1614 and suppressed in 1789, served briefly as a barracks and textile mill before becoming a hospice for those with incurable diseases (1795-1860), a military hospital (1860-1968), a school of architecture (1970-90), an artists' squat (1990-92), and was then abandoned before being converted by the government into an international centre for reception and exchange offering 81 residences and studios to artists visiting Paris (2004).[220]

217 Criterion (iv) is: 'to be an outstanding example of a type of building, architectural or technological ensemble or landscape which illustrates (a) significant stage(s) in human history'. About Fontenay, see: <http://whc.unesco.org/en/list/165>.

218 Coomans, 'Identity Ambivalences of Monastic Heritage'; Jonvaux, 'Patrimonialisation des monastères'.

219 Decavele et al., *De Oude Abdij van Drongen*.

220 The website states that during the restoration 'a commitment was taken to attach the same importance to a tag by Corben (an artist who later became famous after staying at the squat in the 1990s) dating from 1991 as to a seventeenth-century doorframe leading into the parlour or metal structures dating from the industrial era' <http://www.centre-les-recollets.com/>.

Contrasting with these two examples, the case of the Abbey of La Maigrauge (or Magerau) near Fribourg in Switzerland is quite exceptional: occupied continuously by the same community of Cistercian nuns since its foundation in 1255, the abbey includes movable heritage and archives that are centuries-old.[221]

***

Monastic architectural complexes organised around cloisters, often in remarkable locations, have a particular potential when it comes to adaptive reuse projects. Explicit heritage ambitions are therefore essential to the success of any adaptive reuse project. The only way to understand their complex cultural and historical significance is to contextualise the buildings from a holistic perspective that includes every aspect of architectural and historical study, as well as spiritual and intangible dimensions.

Heritage value assessments of monastic architectural complexes will consider each monastic complex as a whole, with the dense spatio-temporal layering that results from the daily life of religious communities that evolved between tradition and reformation, adapting generation after generation to a changing society. The afterlife of religious houses could include several layers of successive reuses, which are part of the history of the place too.

221 Delétra-Varreras, *L'Abbaye de La Maigrauge*.

Fig. 104. Benedictine abbey of Admont (Austria), designed by architect Joseph Hueber, 1776.
[© Lev Tsimbler/ 123RF Stock Photo]

BIBLIOGRAPHY

Adriaenssens, Ivo; Booth, Kevin and De Clus, Lieselotte. *Converted Monasteries / Monastères convertis / Herbestemde kloosters*. Tienen: Sien, 2008.

Albani, Francesca. 'New Lives for Deconsacrated Churches. Symbolic Values and the Identity of the Place' in: Donatella Fiorani, Loughlin Kealy and Stefano Francesco Musso, eds. *Conservation – Adaptation. Keeping Alive the Spirit of the Place. Adaptive Reuse of Heritage with Symbolic Value*. EAAE Transactions on Architectural Education 65. Hasselt: European Association for Architectural Education, 2017, 11-16.

Alford, Élisée and De la Croix, Paul-Marie. 'L'ordre du Carmel' in: Gabriel Le Bras, ed. *Les ordres religieux. La vie et l'art*. Paris: Flammarion, 1980, vol. 2, 139-225.

Altermatt, Urs, De Maeyer, Jand and Metzger, Franziska (eds). *Religious Institutes and Catholic Culture in 19th- and 20th-Century Europe*. KADOC Studies on Relgion, Culture and Society 13, Leuven. UPL 2014.

Álvaro Zamora, Maria Isabel; Ibáñez Fernández, Javier and Criado Mainar, Jesús, eds. *La arquitectura jesuítica. Actas del Simposio Internacional celebrado en Zaragoza del 9 al 11 de diciembre de 2010*. Zaragoza: Institución Fernando el Católico, 2012.

André, Louis. 'La papeterie des Mongolfier à Fontenay au XIXe siècle'. *Annales de Bourgogne*, 58 (1986), 29-44.

Anstett, Peter. *Kloster Maulbronn*. Munich: Deutscher Kunstverlag, 1989.

Aston, Mick. *Monasteries in the Landscape*. New ed. Stroud: Amberly Publishings, 2009.

Auberger, Jean-Baptiste. *L'unanimité cistercienne primitive, mythe ou réalité?* Studia et documenta 3. Achel: Cîteaux commentarii cistercienses, 1986.

Aubert, Denis. 'Habiter des maisons'. *Art d'Église*, 156 (1971), 218-224.

Aubert, Marcel and de Maillé, Marie-Jeanne. *L'architecture cistercienne en France*. Paris: Les éditions d'art et d'histoire, 1943, 2 vol.

Augustin. *Œuvres complètes de saint Augustin*. Translation by Father Raulx. Bar-le-Duc: Guérin, 1864.

Barnet, Peter and Wu, Nancy. *The Cloisters. Medieval Art and Architecture*. New York: MetPublications, 2005.

Baud, Anne. *Cluny, un grand chantier médiéval au cœur de l'Europe*. Paris: Picard, 2003.

Bauer, Hermann and Bauer, Anna. *Klöster in Bayern. Eine Kunst- und Kulturgeschichte der Klöster in Oberbayern, Niederbayern und der Oberpfalz*. Munich: Verlag C.H. Beck, 1985.

Bazin, Germain. *Les Palais de la Foi: le monde des monastères baroques*. Fribourg-Paris: Office du Livre and Vilo, 1980.

Bekaert, Geert. *In een of ander huis. Kerkbouw op een keerpunt* [In one or another house. Church architecture at the crossroad]. The Hague: Lannoo, 1967.

Bellat, Fabien. 'Les monastères en Russie. Des reconversions soviétiques au retour des icônes' in: Luc Noppen, Thomas Coomans and Martin Drouin, eds. *Des couvents en héritage / Religious Houses: A Legacy*. Patrimoine urbain 15. Québec: Presses de l'Université du Québec, 2015, 179-202.

Benedict of Nursia. *St. Benedict's Rule for Monasteries*. Translated from the Latin by Leonard J. Doyle. Collegeville, Minnesota: St John's Abbey, 1948. <http://www.gutenberg.org/ebooks/50040> [accessed November 2017].

Bernard of Clairvaux. *Apology to William of St. Thierry*, 1125 (translation from: <http://sourcebooks.fordham.edu/source/bernard1.asp>).

Betz, Hans Dieter; Browning, Don S.; Janowski, Bernd and Jüngel, Eberhard, eds. *Religion Past and Present: Encyclopaedia of Theology and Religion*. Leiden-Boston: Brill, 2009-2013, 13 vol.

Bijsterveld, Arnoud-Jan. *Do ut des. Gift Giving, Memoria, and Conflict Management in the Medieval Low Countries*. Hilversum: Verloren, 2007.

Binding, Günther and Untermann, Matthias. *Kleine Kunstgeschichte der mittelalterlichen Ordensbaukunst in Deutschland*. 3rd ed. Darmstadt: Wissenschaftliche Buchgesellschaft, 2001.

Birkedal Bruun, Mette, ed. *Cambridge Companion on the Cistercian Order*. Cambridge: Cambridge University Press, 2013.

Birksted, Jan K. *An Architecture of Ineloquence: José Lluis Sert's Carmel de la Paix. A Study in Modern Architecture and Religion*. Farnham: Ashgate, 2013.

Bonde, Sheila; Boyden, Edward and Maines, Clark. 'Centrality and Community: Liturgy and Gothic Chapter Room Design at the Augustinian Abbey of Saint-Jean-des-Vignes, Soissons'. *Gesta*, 29 (1990), 189-213.

Bösel, Richard and Karner, Herbert. *Jesuitenarchitektur in Italien (1540-1773)*. Publikationen des Österreichischen Kulturinstitut in Rom, 7 and 13. Vienna: Verlag der Österreichischen Akademie der Wissenschaften, 1986-2007, 2 vol.

Braunfels, Wolfgang. *Monasteries of Western Europe. The Architecture of the Orders*. London: Thames & Hudson, 1972 [translation of *Abendländische Klosterbaukunst*. Cologne, 1969].

Brittain-Catlin, Timothy; De Maeyer, Jan and Bressani, Martin, eds. *Gothic Revival Worldwide. A.W.N. Pugin's Global Influence*. KADOC Artes 16. Leuven: Leuven University Press, 2016.

Brooke, Christopher. *The Age of the Cloister: The Story of Monastic Life in the Middle Ages*. New York: Hidden Spring, 2002.

Brooks Hedstrom, Darlène L. *The Monastic Landscape of Late Antique Egypt. An Archaeological Reconstruction*. Cambridge: Cambridge University Press, 2017.

Brugués, Jean-Louis. 'La clôture: son sens et son projet dans une vie religieuse'. *17e journée de Fontevraud, 1er juin 2002, basé sur l'Instruction Verbi sponsa, sur la vie contemplative et la clôture des moniales*. Congrégation romaine pour les instituts de vie consacrée et les sociétés de vie apostolique, 13 May 1999: <http://www.med.univ-angers.fr/services/AARP/2002/vie%20monastique.htm> [accessed September 2014].

Bruzelius, Caroline. *Preaching, Building, and Burying. The Friars and the Medieval City*. New Haven - London: Yale University Press, 2014.

Bugner, Monique. *Cadre architectural et vie monastique des Bénédictins de la congrégation de Saint-Maur*. Nogent-le-Roi: Éditions Jacques Laget, 1984.

Burton, Janet and Stöber, Karen, eds. *Women in the Medieval Monastic World*. Medieval Monastic Studies 1. Turnhout: Brepols, 2015.

Buschinger, Danielle and Mathieu, Olivier. *Les Chevaliers teutoniques*. Paris: Ellipses, 2007.

Buyle, Marian; Dehaeck, Sigrid and Deveseleer, Jacques, eds. *L'architecture hospitalière en Belgique*. M&L cahiers 11. Brussels: Monumenten en Landschappen, 2005.

Cabanel, Patrick and Durand, Jean-Dominique, eds. *Le grand exil des congrégations religieuses françaises, 1901-1904*. Paris: Le Cerf, 2005.

Carolingian Culture at Reichenau & St. Gall. Codex Sangallensis 1092: Content and Context. <http://www.stgallplan.org/> [accessed 20 July 2017].

Cassanelli, Roberto and López-Tello Garcia, Eduardo, eds. *Saint Benoît et son héritage artistique*. Paris: Cerf, 2009 [translation of *Benedetto. L'eredità artistica*. Milan: Jaca Books, 2007].

Cassidy-Welch, Megan. *Monastic Spaces and their Meanings: Thirteenth-Century English Cistercian Monasteries*. Medieval Church Studies 1. Turnhout: Brepols, 2001.

Chéry, Henri-Charles. 'Les Dominicains' in: Gabriel Le Bras, ed. *Les ordres religieux. La vie et l'art*. Paris: Flammarion, 1980, vol. 2, 374-529.

Chevrefils Desbiolles, Yves. *L'Abbaye d'Ardenne: histoires du XIIe au XIXe siècle*. Caen: IMEC éditeur, 2007.

Clement, Theo; Ghobert, Jules and Huart, Camille. *Les anciennes constructions rurales et les petites constructions des béguinages en Belgique*. Brussels: Goossens, 1914-1919, 4 vol.

Cocheril, Maur. 'Les ordres militaires et hospitaliers' in: Gabriel Le Bras, ed. *Les ordres religieux. La vie et l'art*. Paris: Flammarion, 1979, vol. 1, 655-727.

Cocheril, Maur. 'L'ordre canonial' in: Gabriel Le Bras, ed. *Les ordres religieux. La vie et l'art*. Paris: Flammarion, 1980, vol. 2, 7-137.

Conant, Kenneth John. *Carolingian and Romanesque Architecture, 800 to 1200*. New Haven - London: Yale University Press, 1992.

Conant, Kenneth John. *Cluny, les églises et la maison du chef d'ordre*. Cambridge, Mass.: The Mediaeval Academy of America, 1968.

Converted Churches. Antwerp: Tectum publishers, 2007.

Coomans, Thomas. *L'abbaye de Villers-en-Brabant. Construction, configuration et signification d'une abbaye cistercienne gothique*. Studia et documenta 11. Brussels: Éditions Racine; Brecht: Cîteaux Commentarii cistercienses, 2000.

Coomans, Thomas. 'L'architecture médiévale des ordres mendiants (Franciscains, Dominicains, Carmes et Augustins) en Belgique et aux Pays-Bas'. *Revue belge d'archéologie et d'histoire de l'art*, 70 (2001), 3-111.

Coomans, Thomas, ed. *La Ramée. Une abbaye cistercienne en Brabant wallon*. Brussels: Éditions Racine, 2002.

Coomans, Thomas. 'L'église Saint-Jean-Berchmans du Collège Saint-Michel (1908-1912), au cœur d'un projet pédagogique et identitaire jésuite' in: Bernard Stenuit, ed. *Les collèges jésuites de Bruxelles: histoire et pédagogie (1604-1835-1905-2005)*. Brussels: Éditions Lessius, 2005, 399-430.

Coomans, Thomas. 'Reuse of Sacred Places: Perspectives for a Long Tradition' in: Thomas Coomans, Herman De Dijn, Jan De Maeyer, Rajesh Heynickx and Bart Verschaffel, eds. *Loci Sacri. Understanding Sacred Places*. KADOC Studies on Religion, Culture and Society 9. Leuven: Leuven University Press, 2012, 221-241.

Coomans, Thomas. 'Cistercian Architecture or Architecture of the Cistercians?' in: Mette Birkedal Bruun, ed. *Cambridge Companion on the Cistercian Order*. Cambridge: Cambridge University Press, 2013, 151-169.

Coomans, Thomas. 'Identity Ambivalences of Monastic Heritage and International Networks: The Case of the Cistercians and Trappists' in: Dirk Callebaut, Jan Marík and Jana Maríkova, eds. *Heritage Reinvents Europe. Proceedings of the International Conference, Ename 17-19 March 2011*. EAC Occasional Paper 7. Jambes: Europae Archaeologiae Consilium, 2013, 93-100.

Coomans, Thomas. 'Heritagization of an Abbey Ruin: The Use of Villers Abbey after the Monks Left' in: Luc Noppen, Thomas Coomans and Martin Drouin, eds. *Des couvents en héritage / Religious Houses: A Legacy*. Patrimoine urbain 15. Québec: Presses de l'Université du Québec, 2015, 301-325 [revised version of 'From Romanticism to New Age: The Evolving Perception of a Church Ruin'. *Téoros. Revue de recherche en tourisme*, 24 (2005) 2, 47-57].

Coomans, Thomas. 'L'ordre autour du cloître: l'architecture des abbayes et des couvents entre tradition, réformes et réaffectations' in: Luc Noppen, Thomas Coomans and Martin Drouin, eds. *Des couvents en héritage / Religious Houses: A Legacy*. Patrimoine urbain 15. Québec: Presses de l'Université du Québec, 2015, 13-109.

Coomans, Thomas. 'Entrevista'. *Revista História da Arte. Série W*. Lisbon: Instituto de História da Arts, 5 (2017), 6-11. <http://revistaharte.fcsh.unl.pt/rhaw5/RHA_W_5.pdf>.

Coomans, Thomas and Bergmans, Anna, eds. *In zuiverheid leven. Het Sint-Agnesbegijnhof van Sint-Truiden: het hof, de kerk, de muurschilderingen*. Relicta monografieën 2. Brussels: VIOE, 2008.

Coomans, Thomas; De Dijn, Herman; De Maeyer, Jan; Heynickx, Rajesh and Verschaffel, Bart, eds. *Loci Sacri. Understanding Sacred Places*. KADOC Studies on Religion, Culture and Society 9. Leuven: Leuven University Press, 2012.

Coppack, Glynn. *Abbeys and Priories*. London: English Heritage, 1990.

Coppack, Glynn. *The White Monks: The Cistercians in Britain, 1228-1540*. Stroud: Tempus, 1998.

Coppack, Glynn. *Fountains Abbey: The Cistercians in Northern England*. Stroud: Tempus, 2003.

Coppack, Glynn and Aston, Mick. *Christ's Poor Men. The Carthusians in England*. Stroud: Tempus, 2002.

Cosse, Jean. 'The Monastery of Saint Andrew at Ottignies / Le monastère Saint-André à Ottignies'. *Art d'Église*, 157 (1971), 225-237.

Craemer, Ulrich. *Das Hospital als Bautyp des Mittelalters*. Stuttgart: Kohlhammer, 1963.

Culot, Maurice and Méade, Martin, eds. *Dom Bellot: moine-architecte, 1876-1944*. Paris: Norma, 1996.

Davril, Anselme. 'Fonctions des cloîtres dans les monastères du Moyen Âge' in: Peter K. Klein, ed. *Der mittelalterliche Kreuzgang. Architektur, Funktion und Programm*. Regensburg: Schnell & Steiner, 2004, 22-26.

Debuyst, Frédéric. 'A Short Dialectic of the "House Monastery" / Petite dialectique du "monastère-maison"'. *Art d'Église*, 157 (1971), 239-256.

Debuyst, Frédéric. 'Contrastes monastiques: Sainte-Marie de La Tourette et Saint-André d'Ottignies'. *Art d'Église*, 170 (1975), 220-226.

Debuyst, Frédéric. *Jean Cosse, architecte: des maisons pour vivre*. Brussels: Art Vie Esprit, 1975.

Debuyst, Frédéric. 'L'église Saint-Étienne à Froidmont (Brabant)'. *Art d'Église*, 179 (1977), 143-148.

Debuyst, Frédéric. 'Monasteries. Places for a New Christian 'Art of Living'? / Les monastères, lieux d'un nouvel 'art de vivre' chrétien?'. *Art d'Église*, 189 (1979), 82-89.

Debuyst, Frédéric. 'The New Chapel at the Monastery of Clerlande. Architect: Jean Cosse (1980) / La nouvelle chapelle de Clerlande'. *Art d'Église*, 193 (1980), 203-205.

Decavele, Johan; De Maeyer, Jan; Quaghebeur, Patricia and Trio, Paul, eds. *De Oude Abdij van Drongen: elf eeuwen geschiedenis*. Drongen-Leuven: De oude Abdij van Drongen - KADOC, 2006.

Delétra-Varreras, Núria. *L'Abbaye de la Maigrauge 1255-2005. 750 ans de vie*. Fribourg: Éditions La Sarine, 2005.

De Maeyer, Jan; Leplae, Sofie and Schmiedl, Joachim, eds. *Religious Institutes in Western Europe in the 19th and 20th Centuries: Historiography, Research and Legal Position*. KADOC Studies on Religion, Culture and Society 2. Leuven: Leuven University Press, 2004.

De Maeyer, Jan and Suenens, Kristien. 'Le patrimoine historique et culturel des instituts religieux en Belgique: les instruments de conservation et de gestion en Communauté flamande' in: Luc Noppen, Thomas Coomans and Martin Drouin, eds. *Des couvents en héritage / Religious Houses: A Legacy*. Patrimoine urbain 15. Québec: Presses de l'Université du Québec, 2015, 329-342.

Demurger, Alain. *Chevaliers du Christ, les ordres religieux-militaires au Moyen Âge*. Paris: Seuil, 2002.

Demurger, Alain. *Les Templiers. Une chevalerie chrétienne au Moyen Âge*. Paris: Seuil, 2005.

Derez, Mark and Verbrugge, Anne. *The Celestine Priory at Leuven. From Monastery to Library*. Leuven: Leuven University Press, 2005.

Devliegher, Luc and Van Biervliet, Lori. 'Vivenkapelle. Een neogotisch kerkdorp in Vlaanderen'. *Biekorf*, 103 (2003), 196-230.

de Voguë, Adalbert. *Saint Benoît: l'homme et l'œuvre*. Vie Monastique 40. Bégrolles-en-Mauges: Abbaye de Bellefontaine, 2001.

Dictionnaire d'histoire et de géographie ecclésiastiques. Turnhout: Brepols, 1912-2015, 31 vol.

Dingemans, P.A.W. *De oude Minderbroeders*. Maastrichts silhouet 12. Maastricht: Stichting Historische Reeks, 1983.

Drouin, Martin. 'La sauvegarde des édifices conventuels et le développement de la conscience patrimoniale au Québec dans les années 1970' in: Luc Noppen, Thomas Coomans and Martin Drouin, eds. *Des couvents en héritage / Religious Houses: A Legacy*. Patrimoine urbain 15. Québec: Presses de l'Université du Québec, 2015, 231-253.

Dunn, Marilynn. *The Emergence of Monasticism: From the Desert Fathers to the Early Middle Ages*. Oxford: Blackwell, 2000.

Durand, Jean-Nicolas-Louis. *Précis des leçons d'architecture données à l'École Polytechnique*. Paris: Bernard, 1802-1805.

Eco, Umberto. *The Name of the Rose*. San Diego: Harcourt, 1983 [translation of: *Il nome della rosa*. Milan: Bompiana, 1980].

Egido López, Teófanes; Burrieza Sánchez, Javier and Revuelta González, Manuel. *Los Jesuitas en España y en el mundo hispánico*. Madrid: Marcial Pons Historia, 2004, 4 vol.

Eichhorn, Herbert. *Der einstige Prämonstratenserkloster und Schlosskomplex Mildenfurth: Entstehung, Nutzung und denkmalpflegerische Konsequenzen*. Arbeitshefte des Thüringischen Landesamtes für Denkmalpflege, n.s. 7. Erfurt, 2002.

Elm, Kaspar and Parisse, Michel, eds. *Doppelklöster und andere Formen der Symbiose männlicher und weiblicher Religiosen in Mittelalter*. Berliner historische Studien 18. Berlin: Duncker & Humbolt, 1992.

Evans, Joan. *Monastic Architecture in France from the Renaissance to the Revolution*. Cambridge: Cambridge University Press, 1964.

Evans, Joan. *Monastic Life at Cluny 910-1157*. Oxford: Oxford University Press, 1968.

Fergusson, Peter and Harrison, Stuart. *Rievaulx Abbey: Community, Architecture, Memory*. New Haven - London: Yale University Press, 2000.

Ferlenga, Alberto and Verde, Paola. *Dom Hans van der Laan, Works and Words*. Amsterdam: Architectura & Natura, 2001.

Fiorani, Donatella; Kealy, Loughlin and Musso, Stefano Francesco, eds. *Conservation – Adaptation. Keeping Alive the Spirit of the Place. Adaptive Reuse of Heritage with Symbolic Value*. EAAE Transactions on Architectural Education 65. Hasselt: European Association for Architectural Education, 2017.

Foucault, Michel. *Surveiller et punir. Naissance de la prison*. Paris: Gallimard, 1975.

Frommel, Sabine and Lecomte, Laurent, eds. *La place du chœur. Architecture et liturgie du Moyen Âge aux Temps modernes*. Paris: Picard - Rome: Campisano Editore, 2012.

Genicot, Luc Francis and Coomans, Thomas. 'Les bâtiments des jésuites à Namur aux XVIIe et XVIIIe siècles' in: *Les jésuites à Namur, 1608-1773. Mélanges publiés à l'occasion des Anniversaires Ignatiens*. Namur: Presses universitaires, 1991, 99-173.

Gesta. Journal of the International Centre for Medieval Art, 12 (1973) 1-2, 1-132 [proceedings of The Cloister Symposium, 1972].

Gilchrist, Roberta. *Gender and Material Culture. The Archaeology of Religious Women*. London - New York: Routledge, 1994.

Gilchrist, Roberta. *Contemplation and Action: The Other Monasticism*. The Archaeology of Medieval Britain 5. Leicester: Leicester University Press, 1995.

Gilchrist, Roberta and Sloane, Barney. *Requiem: The Medieval Monastic Cemetery in Britain*. London: Museum of London Archaeology Service, 2005.

Gleba, Gudrun. *Klosterleben im Mittelalter*. Darmstadt: Wissenschaftliche Buchgesellschaft, 2004.

Gobry, Ivan. *Les moines en Occident*. Paris: Éditions de Guibert and Fayard, 1985-1997, 5 vol.

Gouguenheim, Sylvain. *La réforme grégorienne. De la lutte pour le sacré à la sécularisation du monde*. Paris: Temps Présent, 2010.

Gould, Graham. *The Desert Fathers on Monastic Community*. Oxford: Clarendon, 1993.

Heitz, Carol. *L'architecture religieuse carolingienne. Les formes et leurs fonctions*. Paris: Picard, 1980.

Hélyot, Pierre and Bullot, Maximilien. *Histoire des ordres monastiques religieux et militaires et des congrégations séculières de l'un et de l'autre sexe qui ont esté établies jusqu'à présent*. Paris: J.-B. Coignard, 1714-1719, 8 vol.

Henriques da Silva, Raquel; Silva, Hélia and Mégre, Rita, eds. 'Da Cidade Sacra à Cidade Laica. Dinâmicas urbanas e novas memórias'. *Revista de História da Arte. Serie W*, 5 (2016), 3-319.

Henze, Anton. *La Tourette. The Le Corbusier Monastery*. London: Lund Humphries, 1966.

Hervieu-Léger, Danièle. *Catholicisme, la fin d'un monde*. Paris: Bayard, 2003.

Horn, Walter and Born, Ernest. *The Plan of St. Gall*. California Studies in the History of Art 19. Berkeley - Los Angeles - London: University of California Press, 1979, 3 vol.

Hurel, Odon and Riche, Denyse. *Cluny, de l'abbaye à l'ordre clunisien, Xe-XVIIIe siècle*. Paris: Armand Colin, 2010.

In ander licht. Herbestemming van religieus erfgoed. M&L Cahier 17. Brussels: Ministerie van de Vlaamse Gemeenschap. Afdeling Monumenten & Landschappen, 2009.

Jacobsen, Werner. *Der Klosterplan von St. Gallen und die Karolingische Architektur*. Berlin: Deutscher Verlag für Kunstwissenschaft, 1992.

Jäggi, Carola and Lobbedey, Uwe. 'Kirche und Klausur. Zur Architektur mittelalterlicher Frauenklöster' in: *Krone und Schleier. Kunst aus mittelalterlichen Frauenklöstern*. Munich: Hirmer Verlag, 2005, 88-103.

Johnston, William M., ed. *Encyclopedia of Monasticism*. Chicago-London: Fitzroy Dearborn Publishers, 2000, 2 vol.

Jonvaux, Isabelle. 'Patrimonialisation des monastères en Europe et nouvelles charges symboliques pour les moines' in: Luc Noppen, Thomas Coomans and Martin Drouin, eds. *Des couvents en héritage / Religious Houses: A Legacy*. Patrimoine urbain 15. Québec: Presses de l'Université du Québec, 2015, 435-451.

Keller, David G.R. *Oasis of Wisdom. The Worlds of the Desert Fathers and Mothers*. Collegeville: Liturgical Press, 2005.

Kinder, Terryl N. *Cistercian Europe: Architecture of Contemplation*. Grand Rapids, MI: Eerdmans Publishings, 2002 [translation of *L'Europe cistercienne*. Les formes de la nuit 10. La-Pierre-qui-Vire: Zodiaque, 1997].

Kinder, Terryl N. 'What makes a Site Sacred? Transforming "Place" to "Sacred Space"' in: Thomas Coomans, Herman De Dijn, Jan De Maeyer, Rajesh Heynickx and Bart Verschaffel, eds. *Loci Sacri. Understanding Sacred Places*. KADOC Studies on Religion, Culture and Society 9. Leuven: Leuven University Press, 2012, 194-207.

Kinder, Terryl N. and Cassanelli, Roberto, eds. *The Cistercian Arts from the 12th to the 21st Century*. McGill-Queen's Studies in the History of Religion 2/71. Montreal-Kingston: McGill-Queen's University Press, 2014.

Klaarenbeek, Reinout and Coomans, Thomas. 'Reusing Urban Convents as State Schools in Belgian Towns (1773-1803)'. *Revista de História da Arte. Serie W*, 5 (2016), 31-44.

Klaarenbeek, Reinout and Coomans, Thomas. 'From Guessing to 'Gissing': HisGIS Analysis for Mapping Urban Transformation and Military Reuse of Suppressed Convents in Brussels, Antwerp and Bruges (1773-1860)' in: Ana Plosnić Škarić, ed. *Mapping Urban Changes / Mapiranje urbanih promjena (Conference Mapping urban changes, Dubrovnik, 20-22 September 2017)*. Zagreb: Institute of Art History, 2017, 364-389.

Klein, Peter K., ed. *Der mittelalterliche Kreuzgang. Architektur, Funktion und Programm*. Regensburg: Schnell & Steiner, 2004.

Kometch, Alexeï. *Monastères russes*. Paris: Citadelles et Mazenod, 2001.

Kratzke, Christine. *Das Zisterzienserkloster Dargun in Mecklenburg-Vorpommern. Studien zur Bau- und Kunstgeschichte*. Studien zur internationalen Architektur- und Kunstgeschichte 25. Petersberg: Michael Imhof Verlag, 2004.

Kroll, Lucien. 'The Dominican Monastery at Froidmont (Rixensart) / Le monastère des Dominicains à Froidmont (Rixensart)'. *Art d'Église*, 174 (1976), 326-333.

Krüger, Kristina. *Die romanischen Westbauten in Burgund und Cluny: Untersuchungen zur Funktion einer Bauform*. Berlin: Mann Verlag, 2003.

Kubler, George. *Building the Escorial*. Princeton: Princeton University Press, 1982.

Laboa, Juan María, ed. *The Historical Atlas of Eastern and Western Monasticism*. Collegeville: The Liturgical Press, 2003 [translation: *Atlas Histórico de los Monasterios. El monacato oriental y occidental*. Madrid: San Pablo, 2004].

Lacouture, Jean. *The Jesuits: A Multibiography*. Berkeley: Counterpoint, 1997 [translation of: *Les Jésuites*. Paris: Seuil, 1991].

Lambert, Malcolm. *Medieval Heresy: Popular Movements from the Gregorian Reform to the Reformation*. Oxford: Blackwell, 2002.

L'ancienne abbaye de Floreffe 1121-1996. Namur: Région wallonne, Division du Patrimoine, 1996.

Laudage, Johannes. *Gregorianische Reform und Investiturstreit*. Darmstadt: Wissenschaftliche Buchgesellschaft, 1993.

Lawrence, Clifford Hugh. *The Friars. The Impact of the Early Mendicant Movement on Western Society*. London - New York: Longman, 1994.

Lawrence, Clifford Hugh. *Medieval Monasticism. Forms of Religious Life in Western Europe in the Middle Ages*. 3rd ed. Harlow: Pearson Education, 2001.

Le Bras, Gabriel, ed. *Les ordres religieux. La vie et l'art*. Paris: Flammarion, 1979-1980, 2 vol.

Le Bras, Gabriel. 'Les Chartreux' in: Gabriel Le Bras, ed. *Les ordres religieux. La vie et l'art*. Paris: Flammarion, 1979, vol. 1, 562-653.

Leclercq, Jean. *Bernard of Clairvaux and the Cistercian Spirit*. Kalamazoo, MI: Cistercian Publications, 1976 [translation of: *Saint Bernard et l'esprit cistercien*. Paris: Seuil, 1966].

Lefebvre, Solange, ed. *Le patrimoine religieux du Québec. Éducation et transmission de sens*. Québec: Presses de l'Université Laval, 2009.

Le Goff, Jacques. *Saint Francis of Assisi*. London: Routledge, 2004 [translation of: *Saint François d'Assise*. Paris: Gallimard, 1999].

Lehman, Edgar. *Die Bibliotheksräume der deutschen Klöster in der Zeit des Barock*. Berlin: Deutscher Verlag für Kunstwissenschaft, 1996, 2 vol.

Leistikow, Dankwart. *Ten Centuries of European Hospital Architecture: A Contribution to the History of Hospital Architecture*. Ingelheim am Rhein: Boehringer, 1967 [translation of: *Hospitalbauten in Europa aus zehn Jahrhunderten. Ein Beitrag zur Geschichte des Krankenhausbaues*. Ingelheim am Rhein: Boehringer, 1967].

Lekai, Louis. *The Cistercians. Ideals and Reality*. Kent: Kent State University Press, 1977.

Leroux, Jean-François. 'La prison (XIXe-XXe siècle)' in: Gilles Vilain. *L'abbaye de Clairvaux. Aube*. Itinéraires du Patrimoine, 268. 2nd ed. Langres: D. Guéniot, 2006, 30-43.

Les dominicaines d'Unterlinden. Colmar: Musée d'Unterlinden - Paris: Somogy, 2000, 2 vol.

Lindemann-Marz, Gaby. *Infirmarien - Kranken- und Sterbehäuser der Mönche. Eine architekturhistorische Betrachtung der Infirmariekomplexe nordenglischer Zisterzienserklöster*. Mittelalterstudien 19. Munich: Wilhelm Fink, 2009.

Lobrichon, Guy. *Les moines d'Occident. L'éternité de l'Europe*. Découvertes Gallimard 518. Paris: Gallimard, 2007.

Lockhart, Robin Bruce. *Halfway to Heaven: The Hidden Life of the Carthusians*. Kalamazoo, MI: Cistercian Publications, 1999.

Lombaerde, Piet, ed. *Innovation and Experience in the Early Baroque in the Southern Netherlands: The Case of the Jesuit Church in Antwerp*. Architectura Moderna 6. Turnhout: Brepols Publishers, 2008.

Lucier, Pierre. 'Traditions spirituelles et esprit du lieu' in: Luc Noppen, Thomas Coomans and Martin Drouin, eds. *Des couvents en héritage / Religious Houses: A Legacy.* Patrimoine urbain 15. Québec: Presses de l'Université du Québec, 2015, 379-493.

Magnien, Aline, ed. *Saint-Riquier. Une grande abbaye bénédictine.* Paris: Picard, 2009.

McClendon, Charles B. *The Imperial Abbey of Farfa. Architectural Currents of the Early Middle Ages.* New Haven - London: Yale University Press, 1987.

Melville, Gert; Schneidmüller, Bernd and Weinfurter, Stefan, eds. *Innovationen durch Deuten und Gestalten. Klöster im Mittelalter zwischen Jenseits und Welt.* Klöster als Innovationslabore: Studien und Texte 1. Regensburg: Schnell & Sneider, 2014.

Meyer, Ann R. *Medieval Allegory and the Building of the New Jerusalem.* Cambridge: Brewer, 2003.

Morisset, Lucie K. 'Patrimony, the Concept, the Object, the Memory, and the Palimpsest. A View from the History of Architecture'. *Journal of the Society for the Study of Architecture in Canada,* 35 (2010) 2, 53-62.

Morisset, Lucie K.; Noppen, Luc and Coomans, Thomas, eds. *Quel avenir pour quelles églises? / What Future for Which Churches?* Patrimoine urbain 3. Montréal: Presses de l'Université du Québec, 2006.

Mullins, Edwin. *Cluny: In Search of God's Lost Empire.* New York: Blue Bridge, 2006.

Muñoz Fernández, Ángela. *Beatas y santas neocastellanas: ambivalencias de la religión y politicas correctoras del poder (ss. XIV-XVI).* Madrid: Dirección General de la Mujer, 1994.

Muschiol, Gisela. 'Time and Space: Liturgy and Rite in Female Monasteries of the Middle Ages' in: Jeffrey Hamburger and Susan Marti, eds. *Crown and Veil. Female Monasticism from the Fifth to the Fifteenth Centuries.* New York: Columbia University Press, 2008, 191-206.

Navascués Palacio, Pedro. *Monasterios en España: Arquitectura y Vida Monástica.* Barcelona: Lunwerg Editores, 2000.

Nelissen, Nico. 'Convents in the Netherlands. Strategies for the Future of Monastic Heritage' in: Luc Noppen, Thomas Coomans and Martin Drouin, eds. *Des couvents en héritage / Religious Houses: A Legacy.* Patrimoine urbain 15. Québec: Presses de l'Université du Québec, 2015, 387-410.

New Catholic Encyclopedia. Farmington Hills, MI: Gale Publishing, 2002, 15 vol. (and later supplements).

Nocent, Adrien. *Le renouveau liturgique: une relecture.* Le point théologique 58. Paris: Beauchesne, 1993.

Noppen, Luc and Morisset, Lucie K. *Les églises du Québec. Un patrimoine à réinventer.* Patrimoine urbain 1. Québec: Presses de l'Université du Québec, 2005.

Noppen, Luc and Morisset, Lucie K. '*Heritagization* of Church Buildings. Québec and North American Perspectives' in: Thomas Coomans, Herman De Dijn, Jan De Maeyer, Rajesh Heynickx and Bart Verschaffel, eds. *Loci Sacri. Understanding Sacred Places.* KADOC Studies on Religion, Culture and Society 9. Leuven: Leuven University Press, 2012, 242-255.

Noppen, Luc and Morisset, Lucie K. 'La renaissance des couvents au Québec' in: Luc Noppen, Thomas Coomans and Martin Drouin, eds. *Des couvents en héritage / Religious Houses: A Legacy.* Patrimoine urbain 15. Québec: Presses de l'Université du Québec, 2015, 111-174.

Noppen, Luc; Coomans, Thomas and Drouin, Martin, eds. *Des couvents en héritage / Religious Houses: A Legacy.* Patrimoine urbain 15. Québec: Presses de l'Université du Québec, 2015.

Novoa Portela, Feliciano and De Ayala Martínez, Carlos, eds. *Las Órdines Militares en la Europa Medieval.* Barcelona-Madrid-Mexico: Lunwerg Editores, 2005.

O'Malley, John W. and Bailey, Gauvin Alexander, eds. *The Jesuits and the Arts, 1540-1773.* Philadelphia: Saint Joseph's University Press, 2005 [translation of: Giovanni Sale, ed. *L'art des jésuites.* Paris: Mengès, 2003].

Pacaut, Marcel. *L'Ordre de Cluny (909-1789).* Paris: Fayard, 1986.

Pacaut, Marcel. *Les moines blancs. Histoire de l'ordre de Cîteaux.* Paris: Fayard, 1993.

Padovan, Richard. *Dom Hans van der Laan: Modern Primitive.* Amsterdam: Architectura & Natura Press, 1994.

Papeians de Morchoven, Christian. *L'abbaye de Saint-André Zevenkerken. 1: Un projet ambitieux de dom Gérard van Caloen (1853-1912).* Tielt: Lannoo, 1998.

Plouvier, Martine and Saint-Denis, Alain, eds. *Pour une histoire monumentale de l'abbaye de Cîteaux 1098-1998*. Cîteaux: commentarii cistercienses. Studia et documenta 8. Dijon: Association bourguignonne des sociétés savantes, 1998.

Pouillon, Fernand. *The Stones of the Abbey*. New York: Mariner Books, 1985 [translation of: *Les pierres sauvages*. Paris: Seuil, 1964].

Poulot, Dominique. 'Alexandre Lenoir et le Musée des monuments français' in: Pierre Nora, ed. *Les lieux de mémoire*. Paris: Gallimard, 1997, vol. 1, 1515-1543.

Poutet, Yves. 'Les Frères des Écoles chrétiennes' in: Gabriel Le Bras, ed. *Les ordres religieux. La vie et l'art*. Paris: Flammarion, 1980, vol. 2, 711-735.

Pressouyre, Léon, ed. *L'espace cistercien*. Mémoires de la section d'archéologie et d'histoire de l'art 5. Paris: CTHS, 1994.

Pressouyre, Léon and Benoit, Paul, eds. *L'hydraulique monastique: milieux, réseaux, usages*. Grâne: Créaphis, 1996.

Pressouyre, Léon and Kinder, Terryl N., eds. *Saint Bernard et le monde cistercien*. Paris: CNMHS-Sand, 1990.

Réau, Louis. *Histoire du vandalisme. Les monuments détruits de l'art français*. New ed. Paris: Robert Laffont, 1994.

Rideau, Émile. 'Saint Ignace et la Compagnie de Jésus' in: Gabriel Le Bras, ed. *Les ordres religieux. La vie et l'art*. Paris: Flammarion, 1980, vol. 2, 531-683.

Riegl, Alois. 'The Modern Cult of Monuments: Its Character and Origin'. *Oppositions: A Journal for Ideas and Criticism in Architecture*, 25 (1982), 20-51 [translation of *Der moderne Denkmalkultus, sein Wesen, seine Entstehung*. Vienna, 1903].

Robinson, David, ed. *The Cistercian Abbeys of Britain*. London: Batsford, 2002.

Rousseau, Philip. *Pachomius: The Making of a Community in Fourth-Century Egypt*. Berkeley: University of California Press, 1999.

Rückbrod, Konrad. *Universität und Kollegium. Baugeschichte und Bautyp*. Darmstadt: Wissenschaftliche Buchgesellschaft, 1977.

Ryan, John. *Irish Monasticism: Origins and Early Development*. 3rd ed. Dublin: Four Courts Press, 1992.

Santiago, Luciano P.R. *To Love and to Suffer: The Development of the Religious Congregations for Women in the Spanish Philippines 1565-1898*. Manila: Ateneo de Manila University Press, 2005.

Sapin, Christian. *Les cryptes en France. Pour une approche archéologique, IVe-XIIe siècle*. Paris: Picard, 2014.

Schenkluhn, Wolfgang. *Ordines studentes: Aspekte zur Kirchenarchitektur der Dominikaner und Franciskaner im 13. Jahrhundert*. Berlin: Gebr. Mann Verlag, 1985.

Schenkluhn, Wolfgang. *Architektur der Bettelorden. Die Baukunst der Dominikaner und Franziskaner in Europa*. Darmstadt: Wissenschaftliche Buchgesellschaft, 2000.

Schütz, Bernhard. *Die kirchliche Barockarchitektur in Bayern und Oberschwaben 1580-1780*. Munich: Hirmer, 2000.

Schütz, Bernhard. *Abbayes et monastères d'Europe: histoire, art et architecture*. Paris: Citadelles & Mazenod, 2005.

Sean, Martin. *The Knights Templar: The History & Myths of the Legendary Military Order*. New York: Thunder's Mouth Press, 2005.

Sennhauser, Hans Rodolf. *St. Gallen – Klosterplan und Gozbertbau: zur Rekonstruktion des Gozbertbautes und zur Symbolik des Klosterplanes*. Veröffentlichungen des Instituts für Denkmalpflege an der ETH Zürich 23. Zurich: Hochsch Verlag, 2001.

Sheldrake, Philip. *Spaces for the Sacred: Place, Memory, and Identity*. London: SCM Press, 2001.

Shepherd, E.B.S. 'The Church of the Friars Minors in London'. *Archaeological Journal*, 59 (1902), 238-287.

Simons, Walter. *Cities of Ladies. Beguine Communities in the Medieval Low Countries, 1200-1565*. Philadelphia: University of Pennsylvania Press, 2001.

Snaet, Joris. 'For the Greater Glory of God. Religious Architecture in the Low Countries 1560-1700' in: Krista De Jonge and Koen Ottenheim, eds. *Unity and Discontinuity. Architectural Relations between the Southern and Northern Low Countries (1530-1700)*. Architectura Moderna 5. Turnhout: Brepols, 2007, 251-298.

Socolow, Susan Migden. *The Women of Colonial Latin America*. New Approaches to the Americas. Cambridge: Cambridge University Press, 2000.

Soetens, Claude, ed. *Orval 1926-1948: entre restauration et résurrection*. Louvain-la-Neuve: ARCA, 2001.

Sonthofen, Wolfgang. *Der Deutsche Orden*. Augsburg: Weltbild, 1995.

Sournia, Bernard and Vayssettes, Jean-Louis. *Villeneuve-lès-Avignon. Histoire artistique et monumentale d'une villégiature pontificale*. Cahiers du Patrimoine 72. Paris: Monum, Éditions du Patrimoine, 2006.

Specht, Heidemarie and Andraschek-Holzer, Ralph, eds. *Bettelorden in Mitteleuropa. Geschichte, Kunst, Spiritualität*. Beiträge zur Kirchengeschichte Niederösterreichs 15. St. Pölten: Diözesanarchiv, 2008.

Spijkerman, Patrick E., ed. *Het Rijksarchief Limburg. Een nieuwe huisvesting voor het RAL in Maastricht*. The Hague: Sdu Uitgevers, 1996.

Stehman, Samuel. 'L'aventure du nouveau Saint-John's'. *Art d'Église*, 106 (1959), 145-154.

Stein-Kecks, Heidrun. *Der Kapitelsaal in der mittelalterlichen Klosterbaukunst: Studien zu den Bildprogrammen*. Italienische Forschungen des Kunsthistorischen Institutes in Florenz, Max Planck-Institut 4/4. Munich: Deutscher Kunstverlag, 2004.

Stiegemann, Christoph and Wemhoff Matthias, eds. *799. Kunst und Kultur der Karolingerzeit. Karl der Grosse und Papst Leo III. in Paderborn. Beiträge zum Katalog der Ausstellung Paderborn 1999*. Mainz: Philipp von Zabern, 1999.

Stratford, Neil; Atsma, Hartmut; Bercé, Françoise and Cazes, Quitterie. *Cluny 910-2010 – Onze siècles de rayonnement*. Paris: Éditions du Patrimoine, 2010.

Taylor, Isidore; Nodier, Charles and de Cailleux, Alphonse. *Voyages pittoresques et romantiques dans l'ancienne France*. Paris: Firmin Didot, 1820-1878, 24 vol.

The 1917 Pio-Benedictine Code of Canon Law in English Translation with Extensive Scholarly Apparatus. Ed. by Edward N. Peters. San Francisco: Ignatius Press, 2001.

Thompson, Augustine. *Francis of Assisi: A New Biography*. Ithaca: Cornell University Press, 2012.

Tietz-Strödel, Marion. *Die Fuggerei in Augsburg. Studien zur Entwicklung des sozialen Stiftungsbaus im 15. und 16. Jahrhunderts*. Tübingen: Mohr, 1982.

Toman, Rolf. *Monasteries and Monastic Orders: 2000 Years of Christian Art and Culture*. Potsdam: Ullmann, 2012.

Trachtenberg, Marvin. 'Suger's Miracles, Branner's Bourges: Reflections on "Gothic Architecture" as Medieval Modernism'. *Gesta*, 39 (2000), 183-205.

Tranvouez, Yvon. 'Friches monastiques en longue durée. Les ruines de l'ancienne abbaye de Landévennec, entre réinvestissement religieux et remploi culturel' in: Luc Noppen, Thomas Coomans and Martin Drouin, eds. *Des couvents en héritage / Religious Houses: A Legacy*. Patrimoine urbain 15. Québec: Presses de l'Université du Québec, 2015, 257-282.

Turgeon, Laurier, ed. *Le patrimoine religieux du Québec: entre le culturel et le cultuel*. Patrimoine en mouvement. Québec: Presses de l'Université Laval, 2005.

Turgeon, Laurier, ed. *Spirit of Place: Between Tangible and Intangible Heritage / L'esprit du lieu: entre le patrimoine matériel et immatériel*. Québec: Presses de l'Université Laval, 2009.

Universiteit & Architectuur. Ontwerpen voor de Leidse Universiteit 1600-1900. Leiden: Rijksuniversiteit Leiden, 1979.

Untermann, Matthias. *Forma Ordinis. Die mittelalterliche Baukunst der Zisterzienser*. Munich-Berlin: Deutscher Kunstverlag, 2001.

Uytterhoeven, Rik. *The Groot Begijnhof of Leuven*. Leuven: Leuven University Press, 2000.

Van Aerschot, Suzanne and Heirman, Michiel. *Flemish Beguinages, World Heritage*. Leuven: Davidsfonds, 2001.

Vandenbroeck, Paul, ed. *Le jardin clos de l'âme. L'imaginaire des religieuses dans les Pays-Bas du Sud depuis le XIIIe siècle*. Brussels: Palais des Beaux-Arts, 1994.

van der Meer, Frédéric. *Atlas de l'ordre cistercien*. Paris-Brussels: Éditions Sequoia, 1965.

Van de Vijver, Dirk. 'L'architecture dans les Pays-Bas autrichiens et la Principauté de Liège, ca. 1760-1794' in: *Architecture du XVIIIe siècle en Belgique: baroque tardif, rococo, néo-classicisme*. Brussels: Éditions Racine, 1998, 127-168.

Van Dijck, Maarten and De Maeyer, Jan, eds. *The Economics of Providence: Management, Finances and Patrimony of Religious Orders and Congregations in Europe, 1733 – c 1930 / L'économie de la Providence. La gestion, les finances et le patrimoine des ordres et congrégations religieuses en Europe, 1773 – vers 1930*. KADOC Studies on Religion, Culture and Society 11. Leuven: Leuven University Press, 2012.

Vauchez, André. *Francis of Assisi: The Life and Afterlife of a Medieval Saint*. New Haven - London: Yale University Press, 2013 [translation of: *François d'Assise*. Paris: Fayard, 2009].

Veilleux, Armand. 'What makes a Monastery a Sacred Place?' in: Thomas Coomans, Herman De Dijn, Jan De Maeyer, Rajesh Heynickx and Bart Verschaffel, eds. *Loci Sacri. Understanding Sacred Places*. KADOC Studies on Religion, Culture and Society 9. Leuven: Leuven University Press, 2012, 29-33.

Vergnolle, Éliane. *Saint-Benoît-sur-Loire. L'abbatiale romane*. Paris: Société Française d'Archéologie, 2018.

Verheijen, Luc. *La Règle de Saint Augustin*. 1: *Tradition manuscrite*; 2: *Recherches historiques*. Paris: Études Augustiniennes, 1967.

Viollet-le-Duc, Eugène-Emmanuel. *Dictionnaire raisonné de l'architecture française du XIe au XVIe siècle*. Paris: Bance et Morel, 1854-1868, 10 vol.

Voet, Caroline. *Dom Hans van der Laan: A House for the Mind. A design manual of Roosenberg Abbey*. Antwerp: Flanders Architecture Institute, 2017.

von der Osten-Sacken, Cornelia. *San Lorenzo el Real de el Escorial. Studien zur Baugeschichte und Ikonologie*. Studia iconologia 1. Munich: Mäander, 1979.

Vorreux, Damien. 'Les Franciscains' in: Gabriel Le Bras, ed. *Les ordres religieux. La vie et l'art*. Paris: Flammarion, 1980, vol. 2, 226-373.

Voyé, Liliane. 'The Need and the Search for Sacred Places. A Sociological Perspective' in: Thomas Coomans, Herman De Dijn, Jan De Maeyer, Rajesh Heynickx and Bart Verschaffel, eds. *Loci Sacri. Understanding Sacred Places*. KADOC Studies on Religion, Culture and Society 9. Leuven: Leuven University Press, 2012, 73-91.

Waddell, Chrysogonus. *Cistercian Lay Brothers. Twelfth-Century Usages with Related Texts*. Studia et Documenta 10. Brecht: Cîteaux - Commentarii cistercienses, 2000.

Ward, Benedicta. *The Desert Fathers: Sayings of the Early Christian Monks*. London: Penguin Classic, 2003.

Wilms Floet, Willemijn. *Het hofje. Bouwsteen van de Hollandse stad, 1400-2000*. Nijmegen: Vantilt, 2016.

Wilton-Ely, John. 'The Genesis and Evolution of Fonthill Abbey'. *Architectural History*, 23 (1980), 40-61.

Woodward, George William Otway. *The Dissolution of the Monasteries*. New York: Walker & Co., 1966.

Wyss, Michaël, ed. *Atlas historique de Saint-Denis. Des origines au XVIIIe siècle*. Documents d'archéologie française 59. Paris: Éditions de la maison des sciences de l'homme, 1996.

Young, Victoria. 'A.W.N. Pugin's Mount Saint Bernard Abbey: The International Character of England's Nineteenth-Century Monastic Revival'. *Nineteenth-Century Art Worldwide*, 1 (2002). E-journal: <http://www.19thc-artworldwide.org/spring_02/articles/youn.shtml>.

Websites

<http://edkluz.tumblr.com>.
<http://kadoc.kuleuven.be/relins/be/>.
<https://kleinbegijnhof-gent.wixsite.com>.
<http://lxconventos.cm-lisboa.pt/> [accessed 20 July 2017].
<http://whc.unesco.org/en/list> [accessed 29 July 2017].
<https://www.accr-europe.org>.
<http://www.centre-les-recollets.com/>.
<http://www.chartreuse.org>.
<http://www.frh-europe.org/>.
<http://www.historichotelsofeurope.com>.
<http://www.hotels-francepatrimoine.com/groupe/>.
<http://www.paradores-spain.com/>.
<https://www.pousadas.pt/en/hotel/pousada-evora/reviews> (accessed October 2017).
<http://www.stgallplan.org>.
<https://www.stiftadmont.at/>.

Filmography

Brother Sun, Sister Moon, by Franco Zeffirelli, 1972 [original title: *Fratello Sole, Sorella Luna*].

Into Great Silence, by Philip Gröning, 2005 [original title: *Die große Stille*].

Of Gods and Men, by Xavier Beauvois, 2010 [original title: *Des Hommes et des Dieux*].

The Mission, by Roland Joffé, 1986.

The Name of the Rose, by Jean-Jacques Annaud, 1986 [film adaptation of Eco, *The Name of the Rose*, 1983]

Thérèse, by Alain Cavalier, 1986 [based on Thérèse of Lisieux, *The Story of a Soul*, 1898].

INDEX

Index of Places

Index of Names

COLOPHON

FINAL EDITING
Luc Vints

COPY EDITING
Lieve Claes

LAYOUT
Alexis Vermeylen

TRANSLATION
Laura Bennett

PLANS
Reinout Klaarenbeek
Tine Neskens

AUTHOR
Thomas Coomans (1962) is a Belgian architectural historian and building archaeologist. He holds a PhD in art history and archaeology from the Université Catholique de Louvain (UCL), and is professor at the University of Leuven (KU Leuven), faculty of Engineering Science, department of Architecture and staff member of the advanced master in conservation of historical monuments and sites, at the Raymond Lemaire International Centre for Conservation (RLICC). His teaching includes architectural history, building archaeology, theory and history of conservation.

His fields of research are mediaeval religious architecture, monastic architecture, reception of medieval architecture in the nineteenth century, conservation and adaptive reuse of churches, building archaeology, architectural exchanges between Europe and East Asia, and church architecture in China. He has published 15 books and about 100 articles and book chapters in international publications.

Thomas Coomans is also associate researcher at the Canada research chair on urban heritage (Université du Québec à Montréal), and has been research fellow at Leiden University (Medieval studies), senior research fellow at the Netherlands Institute for Advanced Studies, adjunct assistant professor at The Chinese University of Hong Kong (School of Architecture), and visiting professor at Peking University (School of Archaeology and Museology; and The Peking University Institute for Humanities and Social Sciences).

He is a member of the Royal Flemish Academy of Belgium, the Royal Belgian Academy of Archaeology, ICOMOS scientific committee on Shared Built Heritage, council member of the European network FRH-Future for Religious Heritage, etc. He is the general editor of the series *Architectura Medii Aevi* (Brepols Publisher) and a board member of several international journals: *Bulletin monumental* (Société française d'archéologie), *Built Heritage* (Tongji University), *Cîteaux commentarii cistercienses*, etc.

KADOC
Documentation and Research Centre for Religion, Culture and Society
Vlamingenstraat 39
B - 3000 Leuven
www.kadoc.kuleuven.be

Leuven University Press
Minderbroedersstraat 4
B - 3000 Leuven
www.lup.be